Dreaming God's Dreams:

Unlock Your Destiny by Dreaming God's Dreams for Your Life!

By

David Michael Donnangelo

Xulon ELITE

This book is dedicated to my Father and my Mother:
Frank and Marie Donnangelo.

Who, without their help and support over the years,
this manuscript would not have been created.

Table of Contents

Foreword

I want to personally thank David for his hard work and obedience to bring forth this God Dreaming book.

I had recently been speaking on how God has desires and dreams over us. There are "God" plans for us to walk in. There are "God" plans that will bring forth our destinies. But, too often we are limited in our knowledge and understanding. We are confused as to how to approach or handle something. VOILA!

This book for God dreamers! I was so blessed by the variety of topics addressed, and the creative way in which they were handled and explained. Scripture confirms and brings life to all that is said.

But, beyond that, is the heart of the author. What I have always appreciated in the years I have known David is his humble heart. His heart respects and honors others more highly than himself, and is willingly submitted to working with those in authority. This attitude has, and will, continue to bring great favor.

Enjoy the humble voice that has been raised up to bring light and life to your dreams. Learn and be excited with the new vision God unfolds. May this be a special time of inspiration and revelation for each one that reads.

Enjoy and be blessed!
Trish Groblewski

An Introduction

The first thing we all have to do, to make our dreams really come true, is to realize that: we all have to "Wake Up", perhaps even to the new!

"For God may speak in one way, or in another, Yet man does not perceive it" (Job 33:14, NKJV).

In this book, I do not claim to be a scholar, nor a researcher into the realm of human psyche. Instead, I wish to convey what I learned from direct experience in personal dreaming, as well as, from mentors who have helped me, and leaders who did and some who did not help. Also, I want to share with you what I have been shown from a personal walk filled with the constant guiding hand of the Lord keeping me out of trouble, and guiding me through night revelation. Finally, I want to convey how night revelation keeps me believing in what Jesus spoke to me, and how God's dreams for my life help me not to give up regardless of the opinions of others and the status of their influence. The ultimate goal of this manuscript is to help you walk a walk of "faith" in Jesus in His wonderful realm of night revelation.

"For I know the thoughts that I think toward you, says the LORD, thoughts of peace and not of evil, to give you a future and a hope" (Jeremiah 29:11, NKJV).

It really is true that the Lord wants to help us, even as we sleep, by talking to us through our dreams. The Lord speaks to us in the night, and He plays no favorites to whom he chooses to speak. That is right; the Lord can speak to anyone, those who know Him, and those who do not know him, those who are scoundrels and those who are saints. Sometimes the Lord speaks equally important words to a variety of people, regardless of who you are, what you have accomplished, and what influence you may have.

So why do people not believe God is talking to them in their dreams? Well, the way we perceive "religion" and the tradition we were raised in, as well as the way we believe the Lord actually does talk can impact our belief in dreams. Also, the way we see things differently than God does, and many of the dynamics related to God's reasons for our dream can influence our attitude in not taking dreams seriously. Perhaps, even the mine fields waiting for the dreamer when we are ready to step out and tell our revelation might influence our ability to believe God is speaking to us.

The one thing to remember is that if we encounter problems when we tell people our dreams, encountering problems is sometimes normal.

Although presently, there seems to be a hunger in some people to understand the dreams we dream, during the time when I was first discovering the Lord speaking to me through dreaming, the dynamic was quite different. During that time, the process was riddled with suspicion and bad advice. There were peculiar circumstances that occurred that made it very difficult for people to take seriously dream revelation from Heaven. It was a walk filled with mine fields even from people you would least expect, even from the very people who were supposed to help me.

My question in all of it was: *"What makes people feel that the dreams they receive are not the kind of mental or spiritual "dynamic" they should take seriously? Why do people not believe God is capable of talking to them in their dreams?"*

These questions I want to explore in this book, and answer with this and other Bible verses:

"For God may speak in one way or in another, Yet man does not perceive it. In a dream in a vision of the night, when deep sleep falls upon men, While slumbering on their beds, Then He opens the ears of men, and seals their instruction. In order to turn man from his deeds, and conceal pride from man; He keeps back His soul from the Pit, and his life from perishing by the sword" (Job 33: 14-18, NKJV).

This Bible verse simply means that God does show us, and He does instruct us in the night through dreams we receive from Him. Here is another verse to consider:

"I will bless the LORD who has given me counsel; My heart also instructs me in the night seasons" (Psalm 16:7, NKJV).

Sometimes, we do not know God is speaking to us in the night while we are asleep, or He (God) seals the information and dreams so we cannot remember what He said until an appointed time. Or, perhaps it is hidden just so we do not get prideful, as if we are better than the next person because God is speaking to us. After all, it is God we are talking about who is speaking to us!

In the next few pages, I endeavor, both literally and metaphorically, to give you a revelation of hope and a future of "faith", that you will know, that you know, that you know, that God is speaking to you, and that He wants to bless you and not harm you.

"For I know the thoughts that I think toward you, says the LORD, thoughts of peace and not of evil, to give you a future and a hope" (Jeremiah 29:11, NKJV).

Chapter 1

Everyone Dreams

Everyone dreams. Even if we do not remember our dreams, we most likely still have dreamed something. Many times we simply cannot remember our dreams because that is not what God intended for us. God can seal the dream before we wake, or as we are waking.

"Indeed God speaks once, Or twice, yet no one notices it; In a dream, a vision of the night, when sound sleep falls on men, while they slumber in their beds, then He opens the ears of men, and seals their instruction, that He may turn man aside from his conduct, and keep man from pride; He keeps their souls from the pit and their lives from crossing the River of Death" (Job 33:14-18, NAS).

Other times, we simply have trouble remembering our dreams. To keep it simple, there are many reasons why we cannot remember our dreams that would lead us to believe we are not dreaming when we are asleep. Here are a few to consider:

12 - 03 - 13

1) We possibly do not take dreams seriously; we do not believe that God speaks to us in dreams.

2) Then there are spirits (familiar, familial and generational) that hang around to steal and distract us as we wake. Familiar sprits are ones we are comfortable with and that do not seem out of the ordinary to us; that, in most cases, we are unaware of. Familial spirits, on the other hand, operate by imitating the Holy Spirit but are not the Holy Spirit, and do not serve God. By familial spirits I do not mean ghosts from family members who have passed on; but rather spirits that are familiar with our own ways and habits; that, are servants to our own desires, and often times void of the divine plan God has for us. It is interesting that, in Latin, familiaris means a "household servant". Finally, generational spirits are those "familial" spirits; ones that have been around our family for generations that can, even at times, gain access to us through our own sins; or, the sins of our previous family members. Generational spirits are a kind of intergenerational "familial"- spirits operating inside our family.

3) Sometimes we wake up to alarms, activities, or distracting noises that are happening around us that could cause us not to remember what we just dreamed.

4) Just a simple attitude of apathy - not caring can make us not pay attention, or irregular sleep patterns due to sleeping at odd hours, or what happened that day before we went to sleep, or just daily events that hamper our sense of peace can affect us from remembering what we dreamed.

5) Finally, there is the dynamic of every day practical alarms that go off that wake a person up while they are dreaming. However, I want to address this excuse. God is God, and He does know when the alarm is going to go off. *Amen!*

Many times, I wake up to an alarm only to realize that, I had dreamed, and the very end of the dream is when I woke up to the alarm. So, Jesus does know when the alarm will go off and sometimes watches our schedule of sleep, knowing the alarm was set to go off. In those cases, He gives us a dream to engage in while timing the dream until the very end when we are ready to wake up, and then the alarm rings.

You just need to ask the Lord to place you in His timing, and then you can see the door to this miraculous dimension. Divine timing was, and is a great secret to many accurate prophets and gifted people. They simply have found the "time" door to the Lord by submitting their time to Jesus and allowing Jesus to order their day. So, if we ask the Lord to come and set our personal clocks to His time clock, most often when the clock gets set, many new dimensions of perception we are not familiar with begin to happen in our daily lives.

There is a door to the miraculous waiting for each of us, but in some cases the door can only be seen by being in God's timing. This door to the dreaming of God's dreams is available to us if we press in, and ask the Lord for "wisdom" and revelation in the night.

But, we do have to be willing to ask, and learn, watch, and wait on the Lord to see what He will say to us. *Yes!*

Chapter 2

Dreaming our Life Away?

I think what really struck me about the Lord speaking through dreams (night revelation) is the comparison I saw in the Bible as a book of revelation and teaching, with about one-third of the content being related to dreams, visions, and divine experiences out of the ordinary. Also, about one-third of our lives we rest by sleeping and also dreaming. This has become a very popular point of reference for dream mentors and teachers to make the comparison between the amount of revelation in the Bible related to dreams and the amount of time we typically spend resting (and perhaps dreaming).

About one-third of the Bible are stories linked to dreams, visions, and night revelation - visions of the night. (In some ways the Bible is book of supernatural stories related to making your dreams become reality.)

Throughout the Bible, it teaches us what to do, what not to do, and shows us how to understand that the Bible continues to be in the present even though it had existed in the past, how it exists in the present, and will be expressed in the future; and, how it operates in this time dimension while linked to the past and future (while still in this boundary of time).

In other words: the Bible is a current word from Heaven, existing in the realm of God in the past, present, and future simultaneously because God is not bound by time. ✔

So, a general question about dreaming and it's comparison to the Bible might be this: Are we wasting one-third of our life? Imagine if you had to answer "yes." What if you have wasted time and valuable instruction communicated to you in the night? We sleep one-third of our lives away as a requirement for our rest, so we might as well take advantage of the time and the rest. You do see the comparison do you not?

Since the Bible is the "word" of God, and the "Word" was made flesh, it just could imply that Jesus may very well take night revelation seriously.

"And the Word became flesh and dwelt among us, and we beheld His glory, the glory as of the only begotten of the Father, full of grace and truth"(John 1:14, NKJV).

If, in fact, one-third of the Bible is linked to teaching us through stories that have dreams, visions, and visions in the night; then perhaps, it is more like Jesus is in front of us all our life. By not acknowledging dreams, we can find ourselves relegating night revelation received through dreams to an unimportant dynamic for perhaps these reasons:

First, we may believe that our Bible teachers, pastors, and leaders in our churches are sufficient enough to give us understanding, and therefore do not take our own night revelation seriously. Granted, our leaders are certainly well equipped to teach us in most all cases, but this is where the battle over revelation begins: that we perhaps do not believe Jesus would speak to us personally the same way perhaps our pastors, or elders, or mentors are being spoken to by Him. Of course, that is assuming our leaders do hear from God.

Now on the other extreme, there are streams of ministries, and groups that everything they say is: "Jesus said this, Jesus said that to me, the Lord says this, and the Lord says that." This sounds good, but when it is continuous and so spontaneous as to not test the revelation and motivating spirits behind the information being given, then we need to seriously ask ourselves: *"why are people telling everyone God said this, and that Jesus told me to wear this and that, or to eat this and that; when, although the communication is important to each individual, their private revelation is for them and not exactly for the benefit of many, or a corporate body?" What is the motive behind revealing such information?*

In other words, it is always good to hear from the Lord, but you should ask yourself: *"who am I hearing from?"* Familiar spirits, familial spirits and generational spirits, as well as, the thoughts of others can impact your revelations. An example in the Bible when Jesus did perceive the thoughts of others (the Pharisees) is listed here:

"But when Jesus perceived their thoughts, He answered and said to them, "Why are you reasoning in your hearts?" (Luke 5:22, NKJV)

Other things that can affect what you are hearing in your revelation, or block your ability to know you had a dream, are demons and unclean spirits. The dreams we dream in some instances are not necessarily always from God, because we are in a war against the enemy over revelation from Heaven. (This especially holds true for night revelation that we must ponder and test).

Another reason we perhaps have not taken dreams and dreaming seriously is that we simply have no patience to believe that dreams are relevant. Or, we may even fear the reactions from people if we say we had a dream, and believe we should act on it - that somehow we would discredit ourselves and could damage our reputations.

The devil is in a constant war against us to steal, prevent, twist, and debase our ability to communicate with the Lord, thus the war also enters the arena of our destiny, family, careers, and church. We find ourselves warring to clearly get, keep, and maintain revelation - to walk out revelation from Heaven. So, one of the greatest tricks and weapons of the devil against the church in modern times is to discredit dreams to the point that it is ridiculed if we say we had a dream that we believe we should take seriously. This goes along perfectly with our western-based mindsets (that include Greek teaching, Roman timing and government ideas, and submission to cultural irrelevance).

Modern society, and even the church, often views visions and night revelation - visions of the night as figments of our mind and imagination, attributing them to some natural process. This can remove the idea that dreams can, and do, come from God. (Often times, I wonder if that is some kind of pride that is exalting ourselves, and our intellect over the sovereignty of God in the understanding of dreams.)

It is interesting that the Hebrew mindset (as opposed to the Western one) not only takes dreams seriously, but encourages people to test and evaluate dreams. In many cases, this mindset places such significance in the idea that God could speak to us in dreams that there is a characteristic order, and almost sacredness, to the way a Hebrew mind approaches dream revelation from God.

So, as I pondered the fact that if one-third of the Bible is related to some form of night revelation - visions in the night, dreams, and visions, then what really struck me was that we as human beings, need to be **awake** when we sleep. We sleep and rest because we need to sleep to recharge ourselves about one-third of our day. About one-third of our life is spent sleeping and in most cases, dreaming. So, we need to somehow be awake enough in our dreams to remember what we are dreaming.

We as human beings simply dream at night as a natural process, and it does seem that we actually need to dream to process our thoughts from the day. But, often times many of us may not remember our dreams. We are dreamers in God's dream for us, and we need to remember what we dream both in a literal sense and a metaphorical sense.

So, are we dreaming our life away, or are we taking hold of the moment of time when the light of revelation comes from "eternity" and enters into time during the darkness in the night?

And, are we writing the vision down *(Habakkuk 2:2)*, testing the visions, pondering the revelations, and finally arriving at a point where we walk out our suggested instructions, and in some cases, our actual orders from Jesus? Or, are we actually dreaming our lives away both literally and metaphorically by not paying attention to our dreams.

Chapter 3

Why Does God Talk to Us Through Dreams?

"Hear now my words: If there be a prophet among you, I the Lord will make myself known unto him in a vision, and will speak unto him in a dream" (Num. 12:6, KJV).

So profound are these words; however, not exactly every person is a prophet. But, every person alive can dream and receive a dream from God. Why? Because God created each person! Additionally, if you are a Holy Spirit-filled Christian, you most likely have seen, or gotten impressions from God, that you knew was God speaking to you. He may have even been speaking about the future to you, because the testimony of Jesus is prophesy *(Revelation 19:10)*. All people who are Holy Spirit-filled can prophesy.

And I fell down before his feet to worship him. And he saith unto me, See thou do it not: I am a fellow-servant with thee and with thy brethren that hold the testimony of Jesus: worship God; for the testimony of Jesus is the spirit of prophecy. (Revelation 19:10, ASV)

Pursue love, and desire spiritual gifts, but especially that you may prophesy. (1 Corinthians 14:1, NKJV)

However, not all are called to be actual prophets.

So, why is it so hard to understand what the Lord is saying through our dreams? Could it be there is an actual deliberate reason the Lord makes us search the matter out, and does not make it easy? Is there a reason He uses our dreams to speak to us?

> *"For My thoughts are not your thoughts,*
> *Nor are your ways My ways," says the LORD.*
> *"For as the heavens are higher than the earth,*
> *So are My ways higher than your ways,*
> *And My thoughts than your thoughts"*
> *(Isaiah 55:8-9, NKJV).*

Some reasons <u>to consider</u> why God talks to us through dreams, and why we may be called to search for, and search out God's revelation in our dreams:

1) One thing we have to remember is that God (Father), Jesus, and the Holy Spirit are essentially <u>Spirit</u>. And, dreams are not exactly in the physical either. Even more important to remember is that God is God! God can do whatever God wants to do! So, if God wants to talk to us in a dream, God is going to talk to us in a dream! That pretty much says it all. God created us: His thoughts are not our thoughts, nor are His ways our ways in many ways. We simply often are, way too centric (*"It's all about us"*), forgetting that our thoughts, actions, and even beliefs shape our destiny, as well as, affect others even when we do not know it. But, our own thoughts may not be God's thoughts.

God is an unbound, Holy God - unique even unto Himself. He is Spirit and functions through the Holy Spirit. He is Omnipresent and Omnipotent. Unlimited power is God, unlimited love is God, unlimited intelligence and wisdom is God, unlimited light is God, because He is God. So, the one thing we have to remember is that God (Father), Jesus, and the Holy Spirit are essentially <u>Spirit</u>.

There are several ways to understand dreams as thought processes of communication in the <u>Spirit</u>. Or, there are several ways to come to an understanding of "spirit". In one dimension, dreams are spirit in thought form, and many dreams do come from the Holy Spirit; although, some of our dreams do come from simply our own thoughts and emotions working out things in the night from our daily lives.

In remembering that <u>spirit</u> is what God operates in; then, in another dimension, we also need to remember that we really do not understand the dynamics of spirit, no matter how much education and direct experience we have. We also need to remember God is God. For instance, how does the "Word" of God spoken from Heaven manifest a planet, how does His "Word" create the Heavens and the Earth, or unlimited vastness of space, or even atoms? So, the dreams coming from Heaven and the Holy Spirit may be harder to understand than what our limited minds can perceive, and dreams may be filled with unperceived information.

Dreams of the spirit have a dimension to them, also a timing to them, and what we dreamed in the spirit in the past, may also be important in the present. However, the same dreams may have even more revelation in a different dimension, with a more current revelatory meaning in the future, all from the same dream. God is not bound by time, not even bound by spirit; although, He is essentially spirit, and allows us to understand spirit by talking to us in the spirit.

2) Dreams are a way God can talk to us because we have a tendency to prioritize our time and desires. So when we are asleep, God simply does not have to make an appointment to see us. We have no ability to prevent God from talking to us. Our human nature is not in the way, and we are left open to His instruction and communications. When we are resting and sleeping, we are not distracted, or able to say no to God.

3) As stated earlier, God is God! God can do what God wants to do because He is God! For some of us, that really can make us uncomfortable, even argumentative to realize; that, at any given moment in time, God can show up and invade our space! People like their space, and their way, but God's way is not our way.

For my thoughts are not your thoughts, neither are your ways my ways, saith the LORD. For as the heavens are higher than the earth, so are my ways higher than your ways, and my thoughts than your thoughts (Isaiah 55:8-9, KJV).

So, it's always good to remember that God is God, and if He wants to invade your space, He just may. If He wants to give us a dream He will do what He wants to do because He is God. And, nothing you can say, do, think, rationalize, or believe will change the fact that God is who He is.

I am that I am (Ehyeh asher ehyeh) He says! in Exodus 3:14.

Hayah is translated to imply a past tense or the meaning "existed" or "was" in Hebrew; while, "*Ehyeh*" is the first person implying present. *Ehyeh asher ehyeh* can be interpreted to mean *I am that I am*, though according to certain interpretations it more literally translates as "I-shall-be that I-shall-be which implies future.

So when God says I am that I am, He "is"! In other words: God reveals His name as past, present, and future all at the same time, stating His authority, demonstrating HE IS! That should give us a clue that God is God!

4) But, another <u>very important dynamic</u> that is <u>critical to understand</u> is: the enemy is constantly trying to make the "saints" forget that Jesus defeated him. That's right, **Jesus defeated Satan**, and Jesus even boldly went to hell to announce His resurrection to the shock of all the hosts of Hell. Not to make light of the seriousness of Hell; but, just imagine the look on their faces when Jesus showed up there, not to mention their discomfort metaphorically speaking.

So, <u>We need</u> to <u>understand</u> some of the dynamics (namely the spiritual war between Heaven and Hell) that may interfere with what God can say to us; and, <u>why He may speak the way He does</u> to us in our dreams; and, how dreams could be playing a part in the dynamic of this war. (An entire book could be devoted to this; however, here is the key idea that is critical to understand, in order to help us develop a mind receptive to the call of the Lord.)

Satan has no power over Jesus, no hold, and no ability to do anything but be reminded he was, and **is defeated**. He plays a game to defile the saints, steal from them, kill them because he hates Jesus. He plays a chess game against the saints of the most High God trying to wear them down to make them quit. Only his game is not a game at all. What Satan does is for keeps and is pure evil because of his hatred and contempt for God.

And, Satan does not play fare because he is the deceiver. Satan hates Jesus because **Jesus defeated him**, and Jesus showed us the way to taking back the dominion of the earth surrendered to Satan by Adam and Eve when Satan tempted Adam and Eve in the garden by lying to them.

It was all a big lie of Satan that fooled Adam and Eve; baiting them through their own curiosity of what was outside their assigned boundary, and by fooling them to believe they should not trust God. Satan stole the dominion that was the inheritance of Adam and Eve. Sounds familiar doesn't it? But, Jesus was the second Adam and was not about to be defiled by the same lies of Lucifer. **Jesus defeated Satan!**

However, the devil is constantly trying to make us forget of his defeat. He was defeated; because, if he had known what would happen when the Lamb of God was slain for the remission of humanities sins, he would have never prompted the powers that be to allow Jesus to be killed. Thus, we are always in a battle against the hosts of hell till the day the Angel of the Lord, having the key to the Abyss, and holding in his hand a great chain, binds and casts Lucifer into the pit and the lake of fire *(Revelation 20: 2-3)*. Thus, there comes the warfare that is a real dynamic.

Look at it, perhaps in terms of a real war like D-Day, you know, when the war was theorized as won - D-Day: It was the Beginning of the End for Nazi Germany. Some of the most intense battles occurred after D-Day and the weeks that followed. Same holds true, when the Divine Day of the Salvation of mankind occurred (D Day), the Day Jesus consecrated mankind to his Blood on the cross and saved us, the day the war was won, the battle seems to still be going on to clean up the earth and take dominion from that D Day - the day the war was won by Jesus!

All of this is stated to convey; that it is important to understand the war we are in; and that, one of the reasons God - Jesus chooses night revelation is: that is when He can talk to us in secret. Without entering into our dimension of space and time, He speaks without operating in the air. By using spirit, the prince of the air is helpless to know what Jesus said to us. Because Jesus did not talk to us by speaking into the air, but instead, He spoke to us in spirit, the information is not available to the spies and eavesdroppers in the spirit serving Satan, unless we speak into the air what the information was.

Jesus communicates in spirit, reaching us through parables, dark sayings in the night, and a language that is only known to us. It is very important to understand this following statement found in various Bibles about the prince of the air, in order to understand the dynamics of why, one of the ways God speaks to us is through dreams:

in which you once walked according to the course of this world, according to the prince of the power of the air, the spirit who now works in the sons of disobedience (Ephesians 2:2 - NKJV)

in which you once walked, following the course of this world, following the prince of the power of the air, the spirit that is now at work in the sons of disobedience. (Ephesians 2:2 - ESV)

You used to live in sin, just like the rest of the world, obeying the devil — the commander of the powers in the unseen world. He is the spirit at work in the hearts of those who refuse to obey God. (Ephesians 2:2 - NLT)

5) Another reason God speaks to us through dreams is that: the language of dreams is a spirit and mind based language; but, is <u>unique to each of us</u>.

We have different thoughts about our dreams and the symbols in our dreams, based on our own personal perspective from where we come from. Think of your mother. In most families, your mom is honored and is your mother, but is also your father's wife, but perhaps your aunt's sister; and, or, your grandmother's child. The mother is the same, but it is perceived differently from different points of view based on experience and boundary of our life experience.

This same kind of perspective can be applied to a symbol we receive in our dreams. Each of us come from a different life perspective to interpret the symbol. If Jesus wants to talk to you without the enemy knowing what he is saying, Jesus uses your <u>personal dream language </u>to do so. But the enemy does not know your dream language, unless you talk about it out loud into the atmosphere - the air.

6) In considering why God speaks to us through dreams, did it ever occur to you why Jesus uses different methods of communication (including dreams) to speak to us? It could be because He is protecting us from the enemy, preventing the enemy from knowing what is going on, and giving us the advantage to war in the Spirit (in the air) against the devil. It sends the enemy into scattered confusion.

This changing method (to include dreams) even as we prophesy in part, keeps the enemy on the run trying to figure everything out. Consider this:

Wer Lord ist, Qui est seigneur,
Chi è signore, Quem é senhor,
Jesus is Lord!

Did you understand everything that was written? The same is for the language of the Holy Spirit through dreams.

The devil does not know your dream language, and the harder you have to hunt the matter out yourself, the more difficult it is for the enemy to understand what Jesus said to you also. All you have to do is keep is a secret, and do not speak it into the atmosphere unless protected in a gathering of the "saints." Even in that instance, the Lord might not wish for you to tell too many people about what He said.

There is a time and a place under heaven for everything *(Ecclesiastes 3:1)* including dream revelation. So, be vigilant to the Lord. Listen to His voice, and be aware the Lord will speak to you in <u>your own</u> personal dream language. Also, be aware that Jesus may be hiding the information to protect you from the devil through the hunt for its meaning.

So, be prepared to be visited in the night by Jesus, and prepare yourself for the visitation by preparing the "atmosphere" you are in by praying, worshiping, and taking away things in your environment that are not godly. Remove objects, books, and pictures that attract the enemy, and be humble to the Lord. He will marvel you and astound you if your spirit is willing and receptive.

I will bless you with a future filled with hope — a future of success, not of suffering (Jeremiah 29:11, CEV)

Chapter 4

The Behind the Scenes Drama
in the Dream Canvas of Power and LIFE

As stated earlier, there are some critical points to understand, in order to help us develop the mind of a dreamer - a Biblical perspective to the reality that God speaks to us in our dreams. And, what is presented here is all about "sound", and the reality of the drama that unfolds behind the scenes as we position ourselves to receive revelation from Heaven. In some ways, what is being revealed here, and also in chapters five and six, which may surprise you, explains some of the dynamic operating in *(Proverbs 18:21)*; but, it is also critical to understand what is presented here; because, the dreamer of God's dreams can begin to see the potential of speaking into existence the dreams that God gives them for their lives, and the lives of others around them, both metaphorically and literally.

> *Death and life are in the power of the tongue,*
> *And those who love it will eat its fruit.*
> *(Proverbs 18:21, NKJV)*

Words can bring death or life!
Talk too much, and you will eat
everything you say. (Proverbs 18:21, CEV)

Atmosphere is the air (breath of life) in the canvas of possibility. In the dynamic of dreaming, and receiving dream revelation from God, this concept is very critical to understand; because, there is a behind the scenes drama that unfolds between Heaven and Hell in our everyday lives.

Dreams can be God instructing us how to paint, so to speak, on the canvas of possibility to defeat Satan, and bring "joy" to all we come in contact with! Dreams can be God instructing us how to use "sound", to paint with sound, so to speak, on the canvas of possibility.

Air and the atmosphere have a power according to the Bible *(Ephesians 2:2 – NKJV)*; and, Lucifer is the *prince of the power of the air* according to the Bible. Therefore we are in a constant battle over our atmosphere and territories to defeat Satan. Air has power! The Bible says so!

Wherein in time past ye walked according to the course of this world, according to the prince of the power of the air, the spirit that now worketh in the children of disobedience (Ephesians 2:2 – KJV)

Air is a canvas of power and possibility! We are in a constant battle over who will lift up the greatest "sound" in the air, and to whom are we lifting up our devotion. We are in a war over who will be lifted up, Jesus or Satan, and who will dominate (take dominion) of the atmosphere. We are always striving to take dominion in the Earth to take back from Satan what he stole from Adam and Eve; but, often times we do not realize we must take dominion of the atmosphere also.

If the atmosphere is laced with the echo of the enemy's Hell, it is sometimes hard to see Heaven on Earth. But, as we lift up Jesus and change our atmospheres, taking back from the enemy (the prince of the power of the air) the atmosphere (air), we can bring Heaven's atmosphere (the canvas of unlimited possibility) to the earth and open the Heaven over us.

Interesting though; that, opening the Heaven to the canvas of possibility isn't exactly only over us, but an "open heaven" can be around us and in us also because of Jesus in us, as Heaven is already here, and we are battling against Satan and his defilement of the air. The enemy is the prince of the air. In other Bible translations though, they refers to the enemy as: *ruler of the kingdom of the air*. A kingdom in the air means there are forces we do not see, but are clearly there that we war against with the help of Jesus.

In many cases, even our present day places of gathering for the church in the body of Christ are unaware of the war between Heaven and Hell over atmosphere. People sometimes choose to restrict worship and "sound", control its timing, and control its outcome and content. Or, they choose to ritualize the worship through forced legalistic sounds, and unchanging songs - songs people just want to hear to make them feel good.

If gatherings, churches, places of worship would come into an understanding of their ability to change, shift, and break the power of the enemies control over atmosphere, they would be much more incline to allow their worship leaders to sing prophetically, as well as shift their "sound" to confuse the enemy.

Breaking the influence of the enemy in our church atmo-
spheres can cause outbreaks of healing instead of the sickness
that is caused by the enemies hold on the atmosphere.

Strategies to break the hold of Satan in the atmosphere, through worship, can come from Jesus through
night revelations - dreams.

Unfortunately, the enemy is clever, and can mix
his poison in the atmosphere and even in the spiritual
fire, causing a false fire that makes one ill rather than
well. False fire is an ungodly atmosphere of restriction
and sickness that fools many in the church. Some call
this atmosphere that can produce legalistic rules and
restriction "Religion"; but, there is much more to it than
that. It sometimes takes a person with an authentic gift
of discernment from Jesus to be able to clearly define
what is going on; but, generally, all can come into an
understanding of this activity in the spirit, and that
which is being presented here, in order to understand
how, even our dreams, can become defiled by false fire
(literally and metaphorically speaking).

This false atmosphere feels like the Holy Spirit, but
it is a false fire mixed with the spirits of the enemy,
which produces a counterfeiting of the essence of the
fire of Heaven. (It is an intense convicting feeling of
fire, only one wonders; of what, one is being convicted
of)? It is false, and the accuser is mixed with the atmosphere producing a curse. It feels like the fire of the
Holy Spirit, only demons are blowing on the fire and
fueling it right under the noses of the saints in the very
places they worship in church.

When the fire of conviction is mixed with accusation used as
the fuel and an excuse to purify, it can produce a curse and
can produce sickness from the curse.

Even worse, since Lucifer was an anointed cherub in Heaven, his oil mixed with that fire, sometimes fuels some pretty evil stuff hidden in the soup mix. Yes, that's right, Lucifer was anointed, and that should make us realize that there is the "real" anointing of Jesus Christ, and a false anointing that can fuel the fire - fueling and perpetuating the false accusative fire of restrictive legalism; and, what some term "the religious spirit".

Many times there is a war over revelation when this mix of false fire anointing is present, and the war includes opposition to dream revelation, impatience, as well as, an unwillingness to acknowledge night revelation as God speaking. Or, its unctions produce flippant remarks like: "it's important to keep ones feet on the ground, or stop paying attention to such "out there" dreams and visions because they don't really mean anything.

You were the anointed cherub who covers; I established you; You were on the holy mountain of God; You walked back and forth in the midst of fiery stones. (Ezekiel 28:14, NKJV)

Although this verse of *Ezekiel 28:14* is about Satan (the anointed cherub) walking back and forth midst fiery stones on the <u>Holy Mountain in Jerusalem</u>, if we <u>break the influence</u> of the enemy (The covering of the false) in our church (Holy Mountains of God) atmospheres that are mixed with Heaven's fire, it can cause **outbreaks of healing** instead of sickness that is caused by the enemies hold on the atmosphere. **Outbreaks of healing** demonstrate the **miraculous** canvas of possibility - the unlimited power and potential of the atmosphere of the Heaven of Jesus.

The only real caution with worship is to make sure the worship leaders and worship teams are not exalting themselves above the congregations collectively, and the people individually, or even the prompting of Jesus. Lucifer did that, and ended up in a war with the Angels to dominate Heaven's atmosphere, among other things, eventually being cast out of Heaven only to become vile and bitter enough to try to kill, steal, confuse and lie to humanity, and fool mankind into believing doctrines of demons, rather than the saving power of the "prince of peace" who is the ultimate compassionate "Healer" of all.

In order to understand Lucifer's hold on the atmosphere further, an atmosphere that can carry spirits that can disrupt our dreams or make us sick, we need to understand Lucifer a little more. Lucifer is an Angel that has the ultimate vexed spirit of hate, gossip, ridicule, disgust, and debasing through the spreading of lies. Through his hate (vexation) mixed with his knowledge of "sound" (due to him having been the cherub leading worship in heaven); and, his knowledge of "sounds" ability to manipulate and change atmospheres, the enemy pollutes atmospheres, and literally poisons atmospheres through the mixing of "his evil", his brand of toxic choking spirit, birthed out of the hate for Jesus, and contempt of God.

In some places there is a naive unawareness by many who have not understood that Satan is able to manipulate air (their atmosphere), and that he has the ability to corrupt spirit, and even twist revelation coming to us in our dreams while we sleep. (he being the prince of the air). The enemy by just existing, corrupts atmospheres and spirit because he was created with the instruments of Heaven placed in him by God. That's right, the instruments that were originally meant for Heaven, instruments of God's "Glory" (Gold work) were placed into Lucifer by God when God created him. *(Ezekiel 28:13 - KJV) (The Issachar School - GOZ).*

You have been in Eden the garden of God; every precious stone was your covering, the sardius, topaz, and the diamond, the beryl, the onyx, and the jasper, the sapphire, the emerald, and the carbuncle, and gold: the workmanship of your tabrets and of your pipes was prepared in you in the day that you were created. (Ezekiel 28:13 - KJV).

You were in Eden, the garden of God; every precious stone adorned you: ruby, topaz, emerald, chrysolite, onyx, jasper, sapphire, turquoise, and beryl. Gold work of tambourines and of pipes was in you. In the day that you were created they were prepared.(Ezekiel 28:13 - WEB).

That means: the saints of the Most High God torment the devil every time they worship Jesus; because, the instruments of Heaven were placed inside of Lucifer when he was created; and, they begin to vibrate, resonate, and echo the Heavenly sound of Jesus, the sound of God, the sound of healing, the sound of Heaven's Glory which is Jesus as the "saints" worship. The saints of the Most High God can bring the atmosphere of Heaven to earth (the canvas of possibility), and paint with "sound" and decree, a Kingdom of "Glory" that is a totally different picture than what the enemy wants to create, redeeming the land and ushering in the Kingdom of Jesus' – Heaven on Earth.

Thy kingdom come. Thy will be done, as in heaven, so on earth. (Matthew 6:10, ASV)

Ultimately in doing so, our dreams are redeemed by the blood of the lamb, and the "sound" of His "healing grace".

Only the enemy is playing his own tabrets, resonating "his" wind with hate through "his" pipes, playing "his" tambourines of vexation, envy, jealousy, control, bitterness inside him; and, all the attributes opposite from LIFE come out of "his sound". Because Satan resonates with hate, atmospheres sometimes respond to the instruments inside Satan causing environments to be poisoned and defiled, and he is always trying to defile us, including our own places we sleep. He will try to twist our dream revelation and disrupt our communication with God. His goal is to ultimately defile the saints so they cannot hear from God, and understand the "Glory" that is Jesus Christ right inside them.

That is why, when there is sickness in the town, look into the sounds produced in the town.

So, there is not only a constant war over atmosphere, but a constant war inside and around us over dream revelation, even sometimes between the saints; because, the goal of the enemy is to prevent the "Glory" of Jesus Christ who is inside us to manifest - to fool the saints into not realizing the "Glory" of the Kingdom of Heaven is right inside them. And, that "Glory" means Heaven immediately comes to earth if we worship Jesus and let Jesus' "Glory" come out of us.

Because the enemy, and his demons, and fallen Angels hate, and are in pain from the "Glory", the enemy will do anything to try to prevent new Holy Spirit-filled "sounds" from manifesting, and even new revelation through dreaming from occurring. The

Devil's goal is to prevent the "Glory" of Jesus inside you from manifesting, even lying to you that it does not exist.

As stated earlier, atmospheric communication is a dynamic many people don't understand. And, many people do not understand how the war over the atmosphere is related to dreaming. The devil waits for the "saints" to speak into the air, even to speak the secrets received from God through their dreams in order to steal destinies; and, by hoping the saints will speak out loud things that will curse themselves and others, even going so far as to unction the saints to curse themselves, or curse other saints by getting folk to talk wrong talk. The enemy will try to twist the understanding of incoming revelation from Heaven that may come from our dreams. Perhaps, that one bad dream not interpreted correctly, caused us to speak into the air things we should not have spoken out loud at all?

So, it becomes clearer to us that the air - atmosphere is the canvas of creative potential. Especially, if the canvas to paint on is Heavens canvas – Heaven's atmosphere.

So, as we speak into Heavens atmosphere that we create by worshiping Jesus, we paint with our words a picture on the canvas of Heaven that has the potential to manifest, even in multiplication, all that is good from God.

As we speak out loud the name of Jesus into the atmosphere, the testimony of Jesus destroys the atmosphere of the enemy. The worship of Jesus, the name of Jesus, and His Blood terrorizes the enemy.

There is nothing more powerful on earth, and in the Heavens, than the Blood of Jesus. And, there is no greater name in the Heavens than that of "Jesus".

Wherefore also God highly exalted him, and gave unto him the name which is above every name; (Philippians 2:9-10, ASV)

So, now that we understand the war over the air a little better, we can understand why Jesus does not let the Devil know what he is saying to us, and allow the enemy to defile our destinies by spying, and stealing from us from what is being spoken into the air?

Instead, Jesus uses Spirit - the Holy Spirit, to communicate to us in Dreams, which is something the enemy hates - the devil hates and is repelled by the Holy Spirit.

Consider this: in every war, or every successful war, the first thing the Generals do, or the leadership does, is prepare a strategy to take out the communications of their enemy. If there is no communication, the people are isolated from what is really going on, and it allows the enemy to strike without opposition. Or, if the enemy can introduce false information, the enemy may be able to cause confusion to the degree that the army either: trips over itself, or possibly even will attack one another. Similarly, the church, through its belief in the certain traditions of "religious" dynamics and the associated spirits connected with unhealthy "religious" traditions repeated without a real current "word" from God, have handed a portion of the balance of the war over to the enemy. This part of the war is in defeat because some insist that even dreams are not important, and that Jesus will do it all in the war (Jesus will war for us). Sometimes this also happens because some are in opposition to the concepts of the Lord speaking in dreams, fearing that certain dreams are from the devil.

The concept that Jesus will do it all in the spiritual battle is a lie from the pit of hell. It is exactly what the devil wants us to believe. We have to participate and cooperate with Jesus in any way He chooses to communicate to us, even if it is through our dreams.

Imagine getting a song (sound) from Heaven in a dream that would have such force that would run the enemy right out of town because the enemy is being tortured from the sound? Imagine getting this song from various dreams from different people who dreamed the notes to the song.

When the song is put together, it is the exact "sound" and strategy from Heaven to defeat the enemy. What would you think about your dreams if that happened?

Chapter 5

Atmosphere is the Canvas of Creative Potential

Then God said, "Let there be a firmament in the midst of the waters, and let it divide the waters from the waters." Thus God made the firmament, and divided the waters which were under the firmament from the waters which were above the firmament; and it was so. And God called the firmament Heaven. So the evening and the morning were the second day (Genesis 1:6-8, NKJV)

The dream theater (atmosphere) of our minds can also be the movie theater (canvas) of creative potential for our future. The saints of the Most High God "can" bring the atmosphere of Heaven to Earth (the canvas of possibility).

The dreams of the saints of the Most High God that bring the atmosphere of Heaven to earth can be the blueprints for LIFE, and bring into the reality of our lives and our destinies, a kingdom of "Glory" that is a totally different picture than what the enemy wants to create with his "sound," and what the enemy has tried to defile ever since the firmament was created by God.

Redeeming our lives, redeeming the land, and ushering in the kingdom of Jesus' Heaven are not only God's dream for our lives; but, these good things are God's dream in our dreams, as He is the author and writer of our night revelations. So, the dream theater (atmosphere) of our minds is the canvas of creative potential, especially if the canvas is Heaven's canvas and Heaven's atmosphere. In one way of thinking, our "words" aligned with the "Word" or the words from the Bible, are the paints and colors of the Lord, as we paint the picture of our dreams on the canvas of Heaven's atmosphere.

As we speak into our dreams, as we decree into the dream that which was sent from Heaven for our lives, we can create a painting with our words of "faith." This painting will be a picture on the canvas of Heaven's intention for our lives which has the potential to manifest, even multiply. We "can" do this by trusting, believing, and worshiping Jesus. All of this can come from a single dream we receive that is really God's dream for us, if we only would have faith to believe he is speaking to us through dreams.

Of course, not all dreams we have are destiny dreams. But, the simplest dream we receive could be a tiny spark, a divine tweak of correction, a tiny unction to place us into alignment with all that we have been pressing into. As a result of this small dream, everything in our lives can change for the better, and we may even be able to help those around us, even affecting our family, churches, cities, and nations. Again, all of this can occur from a single dream that can be unpacked in the way God wants us to unpack it, in His timing, as God reveals it to us.

And as we speak out loud the name of Jesus into the atmosphere, the testimony of Jesus destroys the atmosphere of the enemy. As God's dreams for our lives are painted in the theater of our mind, soul, and spirit through the Holy Spirit, the Name of Jesus becomes the mortar, the cement of "faith" that holds together the revelation of Heaven for all of us. Only His name and His Blood have the DNA of Eternity in it, and the name of Jesus, and His Blood of Jesus together becomes the supernatural dunamis of possibility.

There is nothing more powerful on Earth and in the Heavens than the Blood of Jesus and the name of Jesus as it is applied to the canvas of possibilities.

Remember, our decrees, prayers, and spoken words are the paint applied to the canvas. The canvas can be Heavens canvas of unlimited possibility, or the canvas produced by the enemy of Jesus, who will use those words (paints) and begin to distort, twist, and ultimately try to paint an entirely different picture than what you were instructed from Heaven to paint.

Atmosphere is a canvas of the miraculous, or it can be defiled by the devil. But, as we worship Jesus and lift Him up, we change our atmospheres in order to paint on the **canvas of miracles** with our words. Changing the atmosphere is only the first step. We must then decree words the Lord tells us to paint with, in order to manifest the kingdom of Heaven on Earth.

Atmosphere has unlimited potential. The color of the paint is as important as the paint itself. How will you use color to paint your painting? What colors will you choose? And how will the colors you choose make others feel? What painting will you paint from the ideas God gives you from the dreams you dream? Will your destiny, or the destiny of others be effected by the paintings you paint?

Chapter 6

The Devil is Not Omniscient!

What I think is important for all of us to understand, and what was pointed out to me as rather important to mention by Pastor Groblewski of NC4 and Grace Network, is that the **devil is not omniscient**. This was also revealed to me by Dr. Heidler and Dr. Pierce of GOZ at The Issachar School. That is a hard thing to grasp. The Devil is Not Omniscient! The devil can only operate legally in our lives <u>if we give him permission</u>.

We sometimes think the enemy is able to be omniscient like God in relation to our dreams. That is not true. Not only does Satan deceive the whole world because he can use any sinful nature of man; but, the devil is deceitful <u>above all things</u>, and he will try to make you think he is omniscient. He is a liar! And, he will try to convince you he is just like God, even in knowing your dreams. He is not. He is a liar!

The devil can only understand things happening on the basis of his minion servants, demons, demi-gods (demons), and fallen Angels operating in the second Heaven (principalities and powers), but he cannot know what Jesus says to us in our dreams, unless we

surrender it into the atmosphere, or we have left ourselves open in the night to be spoken to by the enemy.
The devil was cast out of Heaven as the deceiver of the
whole world.

but they did not prevail, nor was a place found for them in
heaven any longer. So the great dragon was cast out, that
serpent of old, called the Devil and Satan, who deceives the
whole world; he was cast to the earth, and his angels were
cast out with him (Rev:12:8-9, NKJV).

The enemy can however, oppose us if we give him
legal right. If we sin by entering into some form of iniq-
uity not pleasing to Jesus and walk a twisted walk (not
because Jesus is punishing us, but because we fall less
closer and less fuller of His glory– falling short of the
"Glory "that "is" Jesus inside us [short changing our-
selves]). So, by making ourselves unprotected from the
darkness of the devil, we do give the devil legal access
to us. This is seen in the Bible:

Then Jesus said to him, "Away with you, Satan! For it is
written, 'You shall worship the LORD your God, and Him
only you shall serve (Matthew 4:10, NKJV).

In other words, Satan had no ability to make Jesus
sin! The devil had no legal right to Jesus! We give the
enemy access to us by our own fall - by giving him a
kind of legal access to some aspect of our lives; but,
the enemy cannot know your intimate conversations
that occur in your dreams between the Lord and you
unless you have given the enemy access to you, or by
speaking your dreams out loud.

in which you once walked according to the course of this world, according to the prince of the power of the air, the spirit who now works in the sons of disobedience (Ephesians 2:2, NKJV).

If you have ever wondered why, when you are expressing your heart's desires, or telling people what you are building and doing, why sometimes you then engage in opposition? The reason is: that the enemy has access to the information through the air (via familiar, familial, generational and demonic spirits - minions as some would call them). The devil uses spirits serving him to inform him; thus, making him look like he is omniscient like God – Jesus. This can fool the saints, but the devil is the most corrupt of liars and deceivers, and he is not omniscient. However, **Jesus is omniscient!**

The enemy will and can however, attempt to change laws and time. He will war to do that. He will speak against (curse) the Most High and oppress his saints and try to change the set times and the laws that are good, and keep us out of the timing of the Lord to hear from the Lord, and try to capture our time to try to ruin our destinies in Christ Jesus. He will **try to capture our time** by slowing down projects, meetings, important divine meetings destined by God to affect our lives, or by imposing laws - deliberate self-serving laws of those who the enemy uses, that only serve those who create them – self-serving laws, to ware us down and try to ruin our destinies, and our timing in Christ Jesus.

... He shall speak pompous words against the Most High, Shall persecute the saints of the Most High, And shall intend to change times and law. Then the saints shall be given into his hand For a time and times and half a time (Daniel 7:25, NKJV)

But, the devil is <u>not omniscient</u>, and the "saints," by having Jesus in them and bringing forth God's information, in part *(1 Corinthians 13:9)*, keep the enemy on the run - keeping him trying to figure out what is going on. That is how Jesus protects you (us), so you can enter into your destiny He formed for you in His dream for you. As Lou Engle describes it: *"God had a dream about us"*, *"yes that's right,"* *"He had a dream of what we were to be and do, even before we were formed in our mother's womb. He wrapped a body around the Dream - His Dream! We are all God's Dream in body form!"*

We are a dream in action in the earth realm that can do much damage to the enemy and destroy the works of the devil. That is if we are ***dreaming God's dreams.*** By *dreaming God's dreams* for our lives, having Jesus confidentially speaking to us in our dreams, taking the key that unlocks the understanding of our dreams, and acting on what the Lord might speak to us, we can unlock that which the enemy has bound up in our atmosphere and has kept locked. We unlock our destiny by hearing the voice of the Lord through our dreams – a destiny of hope and of LIFE.

For I know the thoughts that I think toward you, says the LORD, thoughts of peace and not of evil, to give you a future and a hope (Jeremiah 29:11, NKJV)

Chapter 7

God's Language Is In Us

Your dream language is unique to you; it is unique to each person. In dreams, Jesus meets us to talk to us in our own language.

And they dreamed a dream both of them, each man his dream, in one night, each man according to the interpretation of his dream, the butler and the baker of the king of Egypt, who were bound in the prison (Genesis 40:5, ASV)

One of the reasons I chose to present dream revelation in the manner of expanding our understanding of revelation from Heaven in the night, and not to create a dictionary of dream symbols, is to try to convey an understanding of the dynamics of "atmosphere" as the canvas of possibility to <u>paint the dreams</u> God gives us, metaphorically speaking. A dream dictionary could possibly limit God by saying a certain symbol means only a few given descriptions of its nature.

I am trying to help each of us understand that Heaven's dreams that come from Heaven's atmosphere, can be unlimited in dimension and timing; and that, our dreams are unique in the way we speak to the Lord and the way He chooses to speak to us.

There is great merit in dream dictionaries, and I do recommend for you to seek out experienced teachers and publishers who have produced types and symbols of the Bible that are particular to your type of dream symbols. Although listing dream symbols is something I may approach in the future, our understanding of those symbols can only be held with value if we are from the same culture. For example, a certain symbol can mean one thing to one person, but something entirely different to another person in a different culture, or even the same culture. So, a good set of helpful dream symbol lists, with suggested meanings of what the symbols mean, are usually meant to help us only if we speak the same language. The key word is "help": to assist us in having a realization of what God may be saying to us through symbols in a dream.

To continue with this thought of symbols and culture, a car for instance, usually represents a means of transportation - the way we get around. As a dream symbol, it can mean a ministry and a business also. This symbol is often in our dreams at one time or another. It is a good example of a symbol that is generally universal, and can have a very similar meaning in all of us.

But, a car is not in the Bible, which is real interesting, but it is a symbol God uses to speak to us. Chariots, horses, and donkeys are in the Bible. So, why does God not use a chariot as a symbol instead of a car? Well, He can; but, the simply answer is because God is speaking to us in our own language based on our life experience, our own culture and vocabulary. Although, if God does use a chariot, horse or donkey, it can have a totally different meaning based on the Biblical dynamic God is approaching us with.

In certain cultures, hugging is acceptable, in some it is required, but in others, it is unacceptable and perhaps offensive or even insulting. What would the context of a hug be in a dream if we found ourselves dreaming about a hugging someone? The meaning would be different in each person's dream that may be from different parts of the world. Although there are common types and symbols that we as dreamers have, based on our boundary of understanding and culture, the same symbols in our dreams the Lord might use to speak to us, may mean one thing to one person, and something different to another.

Certain cultures throughout the world, including our own culture, sometimes do not have Christian dreamers, but that does not stop God from speaking to those people in their own dream language. The only difference is that, the actual time for their understanding, salvation, and revelation that Jesus is the Messiah may be in God's hands.

There have been occurrences when Jesus Himself appears to a non-believer, a person deep in a religion other than the Christian religion. He does appear in dreams and visions. Instances of this are being reported everywhere, even in the Middle East where evangelism has limited access to souls who may be longing to understand what is the truth.

Jesus understands all languages; he is an expert in all languages, including your own personal dream language. Jesus likes to keep His secrets from the enemy to protect us; but, He likes to tell you some of His secrets to help you.

That is another reason why **each person's dream language is their own.** Not only does God honor us by talking to us in our own language, instead of His language, but He wants us protected from the enemy while He is communicating with us. Jesus expresses His love for us by acknowledging our uniqueness as holy by speaking to us and respecting our own culture, language, and make up.

In Hebrew the word "Holy" is *"kadusha,"* or *"kadosh."* A *kadusha, in one translation, is a person* who is living out of the bounds of the normal ordinary. This implies a person whose life that is not bound, and is separated as unique, not like the common. In ancient Hebrew *"kadosh"* literally means "to be set apart for a special purpose."

Jesus treats us all as "Holy;" He sees us all as if we were made by Him as unique, and set apart for a special purpose in Him. **Each person has their own unique dream language** because God has made us all unique and different. God intends for us to be holy. How boring it would be if we all looked the same, acted the same, spoke the same, and wore the same clothes? It would be very confusing, for sure, if all of us spoke the same thing, the same way, in the same language, over and over again. Actually, it would be even more confusing than if we all spoke different languages. That is why each person has their own unique language: their own dream language.

Let us look at this from another angle: the perspective of how the Bible describes what occurs in Heaven with the heavenly angels.

Above it stood the seraphim: each one had six wings; with two he covered his face, and with two he covered his feet, and with two he did fly. And one called out to another and said, "Holy, Holy, Holy, is the LORD of hosts, The whole earth is full of His glory." (Isaiah 6:2 -3, NKJV)

Would the angels be forever crying "*Holy, Holy, Holy,*" in describing the Lord if He were not unique to them? If he were not different, displaying His omniscient character as "Holy" and "Unique", and displaying a different aspect of His "Glory" each time they looked at Him?

What a privilege that would be, to see God as the angels always do. Honestly, could we even be able to handle it in our present understanding?

The angels see no limit to God, no limit to His uniqueness, no limit to His love, no limit to His dimensions, no limit to His dominion, no limit to His dunamis, no sameness in Him unless He chooses to be the same, no limit to who He Is. So the angels never grow tired of crying Holy, Holy, Holy, because they are simply overwhelmed by His Glory, never seeing the same thing unless He wants them to. Instead, they see His omniscient, omnipotent, unending dimensions to His Glory. He is always holy – set apart as unique!

God made us all unique and different. He intends for us to be reflections of His Glory as "holy", set apart for a special purpose in Him. God will speak to us in our own unique dream language because He is God - Jesus - the Holy Spirit. He is also a holy God of Integrity who views every person as unique, and is a God that wants to communicate to us, sometimes through holy (unique) dreams in our own holy (unique) dream language.

Jesus can speak to us all uniquely holy, and differently, in such a way as to not allow each of us to understand each other. He can do this for a season of hidden things, to place things in their own timing, hiding things until their appointed time of discovery or unveiling. This is literally like the unveiling of the veil - that surprise, surprise, surprise, WOW moment.

It is the glory of God to conceal a matter, But the glory of kings is to search out a matter (Proverbs 25: 2, NKJV)

Because each person has their own symbolic language, it is important to understand that when we help people interpret their dreams, we must be cautious to let the dreamer tell us what they feel the symbols in their dream mean. Only then can we get a better understanding of what the Lord might be saying to the dreamer.

There are so many reasons why the Lord speaks to each of us differently in dreams and in real life time. So, another reason God uses our own unique dream language is to corporately bring a confirmation. Often the Lord will speak the same confirming words to us in a dream as the "Word" that is brought forth. The two messages focus on the same thing. That is His way of confirming that <u>He really is involved</u> with what He is doing.

Often each person will bring forth the same information when they are unctioned by a confirming direction of a "word that is being brought forth, but received it differently from the Lord.

All we have to do is use discernment and discretion, and sometimes keep the secrets Jesus tells us as He speaks to us in our own dream language. For His Name and His Spirit and His Glory are also in us, moving us to be holy and set apart. We receive this specialness just from God placing His seeds in us (the DNA of the possibility to our destiny), that was given to us through a dream. That dream is God's dream - **God's language placed in us.**

For I know the plans I have for you," says the LORD. "They are plans for good and not for disaster, to give you a future and a hope (Jeremiah 29:11, NLT).

Chapter 8

Dreams that are in the Bible

As mentioned before, about one-third of the entire
Bible is based on dream and vision revelation.
And, there are approximately 121 mentions of dreams
and visions in the Bible, making up about one-third
of the Bible's content to be prophetic revelation from
Heaven in some form. These dreams and visions are
there for a reason.

They are incredible revelations of communication
from God even in the present, if we can reference them.
They demonstrate God's dream for us. Dreams in the
Bible teach us much, and give us a glimpse to the Lord's
nature of concealing His wisdom in dark sayings. They
teach us we can all dream and have a vision for a better
future of goodness and joy. God wants us to know
our dreams can come true. God wants us to dream
His dreams. Often, the dreams in the Bible are warn-
ings, strategic revelations to move forward, answers
to questions posed to the Lord, instructions for future
time, or encouragement to our destiny. God's dreams
in the Bible are active and alive because the Bible is
alive and active, a living Word of power (Jesus – the

"Word" made flesh) as real today as it was in the past, and as alive with future revelation as it is today.

And the Word became flesh and dwelt among us, and we beheld His glory, the glory as of the only begotten of the Father, full of grace and truth (John 1:14, NKJV)

Now, that is a revelation for today that is past, present, future, and then some. Dreams from God are God speaking to us a rhema "word;" they are the words of the Lord that are current in the present. Our dreams for today are our blueprints for our future, and our dreams for the future are seeds of God's dream that can start today.

Here are some examples of mentions and references to dreams in the Bible:

But God came to Abimelech in a dream by night, and said to him, "Indeed you are a dead man because of the woman whom you have taken, for she is a man's wife. (Genesis 20:3, NKJV)

Then the angel of God said to me in the dream, 'Jacob,' and I said, 'Here I am. *(Genesis 31:11, NKJV)*

But God had come to Laban the Syrian in a dream by night, and said to him, "Be careful that you speak to Jacob neither good nor bad (Genesis 31:24, NKJV)

Soon Joseph had another dream, and again he told his brothers about it. "Listen, I have had another dream," he said. "The sun, moon, and eleven stars bowed low before me. (Genesis 37:9, NKJV)

And they dreamed a dream both of them, each man his dream in one night, each man according to the interpretation of his dream, the butler and the baker of the king of Egypt, which were bound in the prison. (Genesis 40:5, ASV)

But he fell asleep again and had a second dream. This time he saw seven heads of grain, plump and beautiful, growing on a single stalk. (Genesis 41:5, NLT)

As he slept, he dreamed of a stairway that reached from the earth up to heaven. And he saw the angels of God going up and down the stairway (Genesis 28:12, NLT).

Then in my dream, the angel of God said to me, 'Jacob!' And I replied, 'Yes, here I am. (Genesis 31:11, NLT).

Then it came to pass, at the end of two full years, that Pharaoh had a dream; and behold, he stood by the river. (Genesis 41:1, NKJV)

Hear now My words: If there is a prophet among you, I, the LORD, make Myself known to him in a vision; I speak to him in a dream. (Numbers 12:6, NKJV)

At Gibeon the LORD appeared to Solomon in a dream by night; and God said, "Ask! What shall I give you? (1 Kings 3:5, NKJV)

They said again, "Please, Your Majesty. Tell us the dream, and we will tell you what it means. (Daniel 2:7, NLT)

And it shall be as when a hungry man dreameth, and, behold, he eateth; but he awaketh, and his soul is empty: or as when a thirsty man dreameth, and, behold, he drinketh; but he awaketh, and, behold, he is faint, and his soul hath appetite: so shall the multitude of all the nations be, that fight against mount Zion. (Isaiah 29:8, ASV)

While he was sitting on the judgment seat, his wife sent him a message, saying, "Have nothing to do with that righteous Man; for last night I suffered greatly in a dream because of Him." (Matthew 27:19, NASV).

Then, being divinely warned in a dream that they should not return to Herod, they departed for their own country another way. (Matthew 2:12, NKJV)

And it shall come to pass in the last days, says God, That I will pour out of My Spirit on all flesh; Your sons and your daughters shall prophesy, Your young men shall see visions, Your old men shall dream dreams. (Acts 2:17, NKJV)

Amid thoughts from visions of the night, when deep sleep falls on men, (Job 4:13, ESV)

He will fly away like a dream, and not be found; Yes, he will be chased away like a vision of the night. (Job 20:8, NKJV)

And it shall come to pass afterward That I will pour out My Spirit on all flesh; Your sons and your daughters shall prophesy, Your old men shall dream dreams, Your young men shall see visions (Joel 2: 28, NKJV)

he said, "I have had a dream that deeply troubles me, and I must know what it means (Daniel 2:3, NLT)

Then You scare me with dreams And terrify me with visions. (Job 7:14, NKJV)

And it was so, when Gideon heard the telling of the dream, and the interpretation thereof, that he worshipped; and he returned into the camp of Israel, and said, Arise; for Jehovah hath delivered into your hand the host of Midian. (Judges 7:15, ASV)

Then Solomon awoke; and indeed it had been a dream. And he came to Jerusalem and stood before the ark of the covenant of the LORD, offered up burnt offerings, offered peace offerings, and made a feast for all his servants. (1 Kings 3:15)

We can certainly see there are many, many dream references that have been written in the Bible. What is important to understand is that they are there for a reason. We are living dreams of God, and His dream for us is to prosper us and not to harm us. If someone tells you anything different, you need to weigh what they are trying to say (if they believe in God), or what spirit are they really coming from.

For I know the thoughts that I think toward you, saith Jehovah, thoughts of peace, and not of evil, to give you hope in your latter end. (Jeremiah 29:11, ASV)

Chapter 9

Pharisaic Christianity: The Enemy of the Light in the Night!

Not only does Jesus not let the devil know what he is saying to us; but, Jesus has His own ways of doing things with which we can honestly interfere. One of the most common ways the **miraculous realm** of dreams is interfered with, and opposed by the devil, is by using our own limitations and beliefs to create opposition to any demonstration of the **miraculous realm of God**. This means that dreams can be **miraculous!**

The point of this chapter is to allow us to move past our own limitations, past the lies of the enemy, and walk (or dream) in alignment with Jesus in Heaven. This chapter is to help us recognize and align with people (and "their" dreams) who are walking in alignment with Jesus on Earth, instead of just attempting to find a place for our dreams somewhere in our everyday life, or a life that is imposed on us by others, or our own self-created limitations. And, of course, to help us understand and "recognize" the influences that oppose our dreams – the very dreams that can literally be **miraculous**!

For example, quite a while back, I went to a Bible gathering, a kind of church group where the Holy Spirit was very strong. Something had happened that was interesting, and that was not at all the first time I experienced what went on in the gathering. It most likely will not be the last time it may occur either, considering the other places I may go to pray.

When the subject of **miracles** was brought up, I listened to what everyone said, and when it was my turn, I mentioned that:

"we ourselves sometimes do not realize there is a miracle that happens to us every day, if not every hour - I don't think we realize it; that, the dimension of the miraculous is always around us all the time."

It was not long after, about two minutes, when a person in the group who had their turn to speak said: *"I was always taught that it is wrong to talk about miracles, because our focus should be on Jesus."* This precious "saint's" tone was somewhat accusative in a subtle way. They were, in a way assuming that, to talk about and expect miracles was wrong. The person, in a subtle way implied it was immature to look for and talk about miracles. There was unhappiness in the person, and their facial expression was not joyful. They had a vexed kind of spirit that seemed almost violated by the idea that there is a supernatural realm of Heaven (Jesus' Kingdom) accessible to us right now on Earth.

The statements were unhappy with a spirit of disapproval, and there was an echo of taught legalism from a religion of upbringing in their demeanor. In some ways, that brand of understood "religion," although tagged as Christianity, was opposing the miraculous realm of Heaven by implying Christians should be practical and not carried away with such things as Heaven's supernatural realm.

It was obvious that the person was not going to change opinions at that moment, and it seemed that anything presented about looking for the miracles of God in our everyday life seemed in a way an apostasy to them. In all honesty, a spirit of what seemed to be death was all over this saint's spiritual sight, just waiting to be released to kill any demonstration of authority in the miraculous realm of Jesus through the saints. *2-02-13*

Curiously, I really did not think there was anything wrong with expressing one's own opinion; but, because I had heard the same thing said before, several times, almost the very same words, I knew that this issue was something, or some "spirit", that the person was echoing instead of the joyful personality they always display. In fact, the person was a rather friendly kind of person, as were all the other people who I encountered before; who, had expressed the very same paradigm. However, because I knew how nice this person was, I was alerted in my spirit to something that some; perhaps, may not have been, or to this day, are not unaware of. What I was alerted to, what caused a check in my spirit; was, the "spirit" of "religiosity "rooted in/ tradition, or "religion", or what some would term as a Pharisaic type spirit of imposed belief, rooted out of dogmatic beliefs from traditions held - an actual real "spirit" hanging around operating.

It is a bit scary, that this kind of dynamic – "saints" in bondage to spirits sent by hell, most likely from learning and being taught wrong traditions; are in

65

gathered groups; where, the devil is just waiting to use them to kill any move of the Holy Spirit just because they believe everyone should live in the same teachings they have, which in some cases can be helpful to us, but in other cases, the teachings can cause a miserable vexation in the spirit of one's soul. What is interesting is that: most likely, (if) we as Christians would just consider changing with the Lord as He changes, and operate from His guidance and from His spirit (the Holy Spirit), we all would have less trouble allowing miracles to happen in our life. In all practicality though, if the matter of miracles was not brought up, perhaps the display of unhappiness and implied disapproval would not have happened.

The thought had dawned on me: "I wonder why this person wants to go to Heaven? (In reality, I know why Christians want to go to Heaven, because no one wants to go to Hell, but...) I think when they get there, they are going to be very uncomfortable, cause there are Angels, there is Glory, and a perpetual supernatural that is natural, and just everything they opposed about miracles as not normal, is normal in Heaven"; that is, if one were to compare the earth realm to Heaven. So, of course, although I did not say anything, due to the order of authority set in place in that gathering, I did pray for this "saint" of the Most High God, and also prayed that the Lord would remove their unhappy spirit, and that Jesus would have Angels invade their life to rid them of their vexation in order to bring them joy.

Although, this example may seem unusual, it is not the first time I have encountered this experience. It is not unique to me. It happens to me quite often. Especially when I am not known to the people who are presenting, or want to present their dynamic of what

12-2-13

Christianity is and how I should walk it out according to them. Sometimes though, this also occurs even with people I do know. There is always grace, mercy, and patience necessary in all of it. Often times this dynamic is a clue that people are going to be unreceptive, and unappreciative to dream revelation; although, not in all cases.

The point of this story is: until we deal with our own churches, groups, assemblies, house churches, and people in them, and stop patronizing people who are in bondage to their own personal belief structures, who have lived their entire lives cautious and unopened to change; and, until we try to help them; until we stop making our programs geared around pleasing folk who have strong opinions opposing the demonstrations of Jesus' Heavenly realm including dream revelation, instead of getting them delivered, we may not be moving forward in Christ as Jesus may intend us to. (All the while, we are using the excuse that it is Christian to Love and have compassion; while, letting the demonic principality behind what some would term metaphorically the "religion" mindset of Pharisaic legalism that uses these poor saints of God to make their lives miserable, running all over them and us, and even running all over the place in our churches).

This dynamic also includes some leaders who can fall into that category. So, until we actively root out this spirit and get the "saints" in our own churches delivered from the bondage of pharisaic personal legal "religion" and traditions that are misinterpreted, the same spirit that can, at times oppose dream revelation due to being empowered by demons from hell, the Kingdom of God is going to be hard-pressed, but not impossible, just find it harder to enter the earth realm and manifest the true **miraculous** dimensions of Heaven.

making the word of God of no effect through your tradition which you have handed down. And many such things you do" (Mark 7:13, NKJV)

Many loved by God are sometimes, through no fault of their own, like bombs of vexed misery waiting to go off. They are in bondage, duped by the devil, unaware of their own dilemma, or even the blessings of the supernatural that awaits them; and the fact that the Lord might want more for them on earth like it is in Heaven - namely to perform a miracle in the name of Jesus just like Jesus did. Yes, that's right, the very same people oppressed by the enemy, who are time bombs waiting to be used by the devil's agents in the earth - in need of deliverance from spirits, are actually miracles of Heaven waiting to happen. " *Hope never disappoints !*

I tell you the truth, anyone who believes in me will do the same works I have done, and even greater works, because I am going to be with the Father. (John 14:12, NKJV)

"Truly, truly, I say to you, he who believes in Me, the works that I do, he will do also; and greater works than these he will do; because I go to the Father" (John 14:12, NAS)

You can ask for anything in my name, and I will do it, so that the Son can bring glory to the Father. (John 14:13, NKJV)

We all as believers in Jesus, who are Holy Spirit-filled - filled with Jesus' Holy Spirit, are miracles from Heaven waiting to happen!

But, the oppressed of God are worked on by the enemy, and oppressed by this demon principality serving Satan, ruling through it's capping spirit, using spirits and demons of various kinds to affect beliefs in "religion", theologies, rules, and doctrines made by man that are not really the "Truth" of the freedom of the Kingdom of Heaven and of the love of Jesus; but instead, a lie from hell holding the "saints' in bondage to their real identity in Christ. These poor saints are time bombs just waiting to go off in our churches every day.

There is nothing worse that the mind of man creating a doctrine of something that is not the Holy Spirit. The question we need to ask is: "if the mind of men creates these doctrines, theologies, and liturgies using the Bible; then, are their minds (the mind of these men) also the mind of Christ Jesus (do they have the mind of Jesus Christ?), or are their minds attempting to interpret Jesus? ？？

"My thoughts are not your thoughts, nor are your ways My ways,' says the Lord. 'For as the heavens are higher than the earth, so are My ways higher than your ways, And My thoughts than your thoughts." (Isaiah 55:8-9, NKJV)

Until we have the courage to deal with these kinds of vexed bombs of toxic smoke and mirrors from demons that are rooted in personal interpretations of belief in a kind of "religion" that kills, who have come into agreement with the legalism of false rules and unnatural regulations, laced with the terrorism of personal "religion" that borders on superstition, that is other than Heaven's "Truth" and "Kingdom", through no fault of anyone, except repeating the same old, same old, same old ways based on something that is not true; we will be seeing a compromise of the Kingdom which will produce no real transformation, no real Life of Heaven's atmosphere brought to earth, and no real release of the

authority of the **Kingdom of Jesus and His miracles.**
(Philippians 3: 12-16, NKJV).

And, we jeopardize our next generation who will
leave the church, and "are" leaving the church because
of this demon of self-righteous legalism attached to the
various kinds of personal "religious" belief interpretations; and, in some cases, doctrines of demons distracting us from the goal of intimacy with Jesus; which,
just puts us in further bondage, instead of the freedom
which is: Jesus and all the fullness of His Kingdom
which He bought for us with a price.

Although, we can choose, and we do have a choice
who we run with, who we align with, and who we can
trust to do the actual will of God, sometimes we make
some peculiar discussions that simply lead to no fruit
from Heaven. Just like, sometimes we make the wrong
discussion and tell the wrong people our dreams that
we have dreamed.

I think it is important to examine this dynamic in
terms of its perpetuation. Although some would consider certain denominations, prominent church move-
ments and traditional Christianity such as the Catholic
Church as fostering this spirit, a "spirit" that at times can
oppose dream revelation, or even in some cases could
cause some people to believe the Catholic Church is
the cause of this spirit of "religion", or a Pharisaic type
spirituality, as some would term it, this spirit is not
exclusive to the Catholic Church or any one denomination. In fact, one of the most powerful moves of the
Holy Spirit occurred in the Catholic Church known
as the Catholic Charismatic Renewal, which found its
roots from a Catholic spiritual retreat held at Duquesne
University in in 1967 in Pittsburg, Pennsylvania. Just as
Azusa Street, this renewal spawned a movement that
had far reaching effects touching to date over 230 coun-

tries in the world. There are many pastors in Protestant churches that can testify to the fact they had become Holy Spirit- filled in the Catholic Church, or by the prayers and mentoring from Catholic priests. It would be bigoted to assume the Catholic Church is the cause of this spirit, and in all honesty, to put a bit of humor on the subject, this spirit can show up anywhere, in church, in business, in government, in our families; or, of course, the remnant church of Jesus Christ. So, if people really believe this spirit is exclusive to the Catholic Church, they might want to realize; that, there is no exclusivity to the demonization of Christian Churches throughout the world, no matter what denomination they are.

By perpetuation of this "spirit", I mean the actual handing down of this lie from hell that: a person who believes in Jesus Christ, and is Holy Spirit- filled, cannot do the same miracles that Jesus did, if not greater miracles in the name of Jesus. Or, that they should not experience divine intervention in the realm of the miraculous through their dreams that do come from God.

 I tell you the truth, anyone who believes in me will do the *same works I have done, and even greater works, because I am going to be with the Father. (John 14:12, NKJV).*

When you make a statement of belief and faith that you believe in the miraculous realm of Jesus right here and now on earth, you sometimes see that the very people you would least expect, even Christian leaders, react to the statement with an almost vindictive, revenge type attitude, almost wishing that the statement would be proved wrong, and in some instances going about, not the Father's business but the devil's business of trying to prove that the faithful, who believe *John 14:12*

in the Bible - that they can do miracles in the name of Jesus, are wrong and trapped in some sort of apostasy. It is almost comical to think; that, those who believe you cannot see miracles, and do miracles because; perhaps, of some spirit of "false humility", in some ways believe their opinion is greater than what God can do. After all, Jesus was the one who said: *"anyone who believes in me will do the same works I have done, and even greater works"*! *(John 14:12)*

And then, there is of course, the whole idea, that if Jesus can do miracles and is the same yesterday, today, and forever *(Hebrews 13:8)*, why could he not give His "saints" a few dreams for their lives? After all, He did create us, and also created all that is known and unknown.

In all of this, it is important to remember that: Jesus is LOVE!

Point 1: Love is a Solution to the Religion of Man!

Jesus, and a personal relationship with Him is a solution to handling this issue with Love, as more and more people come into the Kingdom. While there develops a separation in our Kingdom relationships (separating the wheat from the tare), where the Holy Spirit of Jesus and His Kingdom literally draws out to expose the hidden activities of the enemy in our most important resource - the Church (the body of Christ) through the dreams we dream from God in Heaven, we need to be vigilant to spot this spirit that wants to steal, kill, and twist any true demonstration of the Kingdom of Jesus on earth. The Love of Jesus is the solution. If we love as we walk, we can prevent all sorts of arguments, accusations through suspicion, and even deal with the not so obvious realm of the spirit (oppressing spirits from the devil) because there really is nothing

72

more potent than the power of the Love of Jesus. The Love of Jesus is paralyzing to the enemy.

Point 2: Why Should We Care?

There are many reasons why we should care about this. Here are a few:

1) The reasoning is simple, the many "saints" who have bought into the lie from the pit of hell by riding the vehicle of "religion" based outside of the actual Kingdom decree of the manifest wisdom of love and light, echoing the "Glory" of Heaven, just don't know there is even a greater GLORY, a greater LOVE to seek after.

2) Some "saints" are coming into agreement with demons they are unaware of, and the doctrine of these demons sent by Satan. Some of the "saints" in many cases, have had all their lives to see beyond the natural and change - to turn around, and become empowered by the real manifest dunamis of the Lord Jesus to do "Greater Works" (John 14:12) than Jesus did. That means, we do have the potential to demonstrate LOVE perhaps even in a greater dimension than we ever have seen, as we strive to echo and look like Jesus and His Love.

3) Many have seen miracles, and what Jesus can do; but, they have a peculiar sense of "false humility" that they cannot do the same thing, or they simply cannot believe they themselves can do miracles in the name of Jesus, as they are continuously afraid and suspicious. And, the enemy comes to confuse them right off the bat, by making them think that the person who is performing miracles, is doing it on their own, in their own

name, and of their own motive instead of in the name of Jesus. This is one of Satan's favorite strategies and deceptions - using the "saints" to accuse each other". Oh, how this accuser, this liar (the devil) has tried to defile the "saints" by accusing people who really want to step out and do ministry in the name of Jesus.

4) Some unfortunate folk have been left to foster, stew in their vexations due to leaderships trying to figure out how to deal with their bondage, faulty leadership not in Kingdom order, or leadership not recognizing there is a problem at all, or even worst of all, they are left by their own brothers and sisters, and family members who have simply let them continue to clean themselves with righteous dirty rags. So, why should we allow the enemy to oppress our brothers and sisters by allowing the enemies helpers - demon's using tools of unhappiness - "misery bombs" of toxic "religious" energy, to go off around our children and the next generation, chasing them out of the church, or chasing off the current to next generation that is willing to change and move into the NEW?

Point 3: The Solution of Love? (A Suggestion in Christ Jesus)

Here is one possible solution to the issue of personal belief, rooted in the wrong interpretation of religious belief that tries to kill the move of the Holy Spirit which is Jesus; and, tries to discredit dream revelation - light in the dark night that is from heaven.

What we need in this hour is a "Bomb Squad" in every Church, every small group, every gathering, we need "Bomb Squads of Love" to isolate, quarantine, contain the "religion" bombs if they go off, or to dismantle them so they don't go off. We need bomb

12-02-13

experts equipped with Jesus' overwhelming Love, that can spot the "religion" terrorist, to pray off of them this spirit using "religion" uninformed of the true Kingdom of Jesus. We need trained experts that can spot the spies working for this demon principality that is feeding false theology into religion. We need a counter terrorist group that can use the Love and authority of Jesus to spot, quarantine, then cast this demon off the "saints", and sometimes out of the "saints" being victimized by Satan who is posing as an Angel of Light *(2 Corinthians 11:14)*. And then, bomb them with "Love" till they are filled up with "Love" and become "Love" bombs themselves.

※
Amen!

The dynamic above is something the dreamer will face, because our own understanding of this spirit of "religion" or even any Pharisaic type Spirits (spirits laced with legalism based on a twisted personal invention of a religious law or tradition) is an enemy of Revelation. Especially new Revelation brought forth from Heaven that can cause change, and expose what the enemy is up to. It is certainly the enemy of dreams from God and the enemy of the dreamer. It is the enemy of the light in the night. You can feel the choking toxic atmosphere of these demons of false theology rooted in personal opinion and collective agreement; which, in some cases is no different than the collective agreement of the secret societies of the past and even present. Why this is important to the dreamer, is because, this evil spirit is literally the enemy of light in the night – revelation from Heaven.

Dreams are mysterious and sometimes just shocking and dark, manifesting sometimes as very dark sayings in the night, and they certainly need proper interpretation. So, because of the very nature of dreams, that God may choose to speak in this manner, there may be opposition to them and any new Revelation of Heaven from the throne of God. The spirit of opinion based on legalistic superstition, laced with opposition to night - revelation is certainly a dynamic that the dreamer needs to know about because God usually does not just speak directly face to face to us as He did with Moses. But, God does speak in dreams, and those who oppose and do not believe He does, may simply not fear the Lord.

> *"I speak with him face to face,*
> *Even plainly, and not in <u>dark sayings</u>;*
> *And he sees the form of the LORD.*
> *Why then were you not afraid*
> *To speak against My servant Moses"*
> *(Numbers 12:8, NKJV)*

But, God has a final say, and God is and ever was, and the dimension of the miraculous is always around us all the time. Because of Jesus, we can live in the spirit of love, life, revelation and freedom which is Jesus and His dream for us. Jesus gives us the keys that unlock that which the enemy has locked and kept bound through his lies and twisting of the practice of personal "religion" in the earth. Religion is a good thing, but the spirit of "religion", (the "religious" spirit, as some would refer to it as, – an actual principality associated with all sorts of oppressive bondage and control) which we have been referring to, that opposes the miraculous of Jesus, is something totally different, and is not from God.

Chapter 10

What is a Night Revelation?
What is a Vision?
What is the Difference?

He made darkness His secret place; His canopy around Him was dark waters And thick clouds of the skies (Psalm 18:11, NKJV).

God has a secret place, a place where He can speak to us that is dark, just like in the night time when we sleep and dream. The dark sayings of God are sometimes very dark because the Lord wants us to see His light in the darkness. So, a dark saying can be a <u>night revelation</u> to us.

A <u>night revelation</u> can be a <u>dream at night</u> that is either revealed when we are asleep, or when we are awake. If we have a night revelation at night when we are awake it is referred to as a vision. However, most of the time, a night revelation is commonly considered or referred to as a dream in the night.

Sometimes, it is called a "dark saying," due to the fact that the night revelation is being delivered symbolically, or like a parable of revelation (light) while we were asleep or awake. Although "dark sayings" can sometimes be very, very, dark and even frightening, "dark sayings" are not only ordinary dreams while we are asleep in the night; they can also be in a category all of their own as <u>very dark</u> messages that shake up, shock, or cause us to be disturbed upon waking up from them.

The mysterious "dark saying" can be interpreted through the help of the Holy Spirit, and there are even those who have been given special gifting's from Jesus to interpret dreams and visions. Daniel was one of these people with a special gift to understand dreams:

because an excellent spirit, and knowledge, and under-standing, interpreting of dreams, and showing of dark sentences, and dissolving of doubts, were found in the same Daniel, whom the king named Belteshazzar. Now let Daniel be called, and he will show the interpretation. (Daniel 5:12, WEB)

But, a <u>night revelation</u> could also be a <u>voice heard as we wake up</u> in the night, an actual communication that comes as we wake up when we are in-between sleeping and waking. Sometimes the communication in the night comes between the time when we are falling asleep and asleep; or, between the times we are waking up and awake.

A <u>vision</u> is an "awake" dream, in a sense, kind of like daydreaming, or something we are seeing; that, we are seeing while we are awake and not asleep.

There are <u>internal visions</u> and <u>external visions</u>. Internal visions are somewhat like daydreams. External visions are more intrusive where the person can actually see things, and believing things are there that are not there in the physical, even to the point of believing they are being transported to an entirely different location because of what they are seeing. (In some cases it can become really miraculous, and the non-physical vision actually manifests, which is sometimes referred to as the term Theophania.)

And Jehovah appeared unto him the same night, and said, I am the God of Abraham thy father. Fear not, for I am with thee, and will bless thee, and multiply thy seed for my servant Abraham's sake. (Genesis 26:24, ASV)

In the contemporary dynamics of Christianity, we sometimes do not take seriously visions in this way, at least to the point of acting on them and believing they are real. We sometimes simply go around telling people we had a vision, but the point of visions is that we usually have an <u>imperative message</u> from God to <u>pay attention</u> to them and <u>act on them</u>, and in most cases, they are immediate revelations to be acted on unless revealed otherwise.

But, notice in this instance, that God himself came to Isaac. We do not know exactly in what form. This passage of *Genesis 26:24*, in various Bibles, does not indicate that Isaac had a vision; however, it implies to some degree that it was God who came to Isaac.

We take seriously Moses, and we know God appeared to Moses, and we often claim Moses was the only person God ever directly appeared to in real life earth time (*Numbers 12:8, NKJV*). However, it is most likely God did come to Isaac in a vision, as described in certain versions of the Bible. But, what if Isaac did not take his vision seriously?

Are visions perhaps made up of some of the characteristics of Heaven's atmosphere? It is an interesting dynamic of interpretation to ponder. In some ways it would explain a lot of the dynamics of stories found in the Bible.

⌐*"That night the* LORD *appeared to Isaac, and said, "I am the God of your father Abraham. Don't be afraid, because I am with you. I will bless you and increase the number of your descendants for my servant Abraham's sake" (Genesis 26:24, NKJV).*⌐ *Awesome God!*

The point of all this is to ask ourselves, "What do we do with our visions in the night? Do we take them seriously, or believe they are not important enough to deal with?"

Usually, when we have visions, or snap-shot pictures appearing to us when we are awake, Jesus is expecting us to do something; to act on what we saw in the <u>immediate,</u> or begin to act on what He gave us. Sometimes it is necessary to give a believer a vision so he or she knows the <u>immediateness of the issue.</u> And yes, <u>one image, one symbol; one picture can speak a thousand words</u> because God is not limited! He is <u>omniscient and omnipotent.</u>

To summarize:

- We can have visions (like a visual movie in the spirit that we see, and experience) while we are awake on our beds, or just simply awake anywhere at any time day or night.
- We can experience night visions which are visions (spiritual visual movies) we see at night.
- We can also have night visions while dreaming (also what some refer to as visions of the night) while we are asleep and dreaming in a dream (a vision while in a dream dreaming).
- We can have dreams while asleep, while we are dreaming (dreaming a dream while we are asleep and having a dream [a dream in a dream]),
- We can simply fall asleep and have a dream.
- Or, we can have a short vision - see a snap-shot picture that speaks a thousand words.

Chapter 11

Exactly How Dark Can a "Dark Saying" in the Night
Really Be?

Sometimes our dreams can get really dark...really, really, dark (dark sayings) in the dark night. Often, when we <u>do have</u> really dark sayings revealed to us, we immediately reject them as something coming from the devil, and we do not want to address them. This is through a false type of righteousness because we are in denial that our dreams could be coming from a source other than God.

But:

He made darkness His secret place; His canopy around Him was dark waters And thick clouds of the skies (Psalm 18:11, NKJV).

If the devil chooses to visit a believer in Christ, a person filled with the Holy Spirit, <u>it is often an unwise move</u>. The intention of the enemy is to cause fear and confusion, to mock, and accuse, and deceive; but, when the Holy Spirit is involved, the dynamic of night revelation takes on a whole new level of warfare. If the Holy Spirit chooses to allow the enemy to reveal his plans, the authority of the dreamer in Christ Jesus is now involved in the dynamic of the dream.

Often we actually receive very, very, dark dreams that seem to be from the devil. In reality, these are allowed to come to us by the Holy Spirit (Jesus) to shock us into action, and to prod, or push us until we do something about it.

Once in a while, we receive a dream that is in black and white. Usually this kind of dream is not from God, but is being allowed to be shown to us by the Holy Spirit in order that we know to be cautious about things which the enemy is planning, or it is being shown to us by God; but, God want us to know it is not of him. Remember that:

"All dreams that are not interpreted are like letters that are not opened and not read." (Dr. Chuck Pierce).

The following dream was given to me by Pastor Trish. What I really like about this dream and the interpretation is that the dreamer (Pastor Trish) refuses to allow the enemy to have his way. Instead, she exercises her authority in Christ Jesus to decree against what she was shown. It is very obvious she has experience in recognizing what was going on, and because this dream is interpreted in her own dream language, I will not place any of my own interpretation into it except to prophesy the outcome - an outcome of light, love, and encouragement.

This dream is a night revelation, a dark saying in the category of being an actual "dark saying" in the night. This is the dream and the advice of Pastor Trish in her own words. (Because of the boundary of her authority given to her by Jesus, this dream has implications for a broader territory in the "body" of Christ than just local).

I had recently been given a dream by a friend of mine. Her dream was that I gave birth to a beautiful baby girl and my son was there helping me. Excited, I knew that what was being revealed by God was the birthing of something new for me in the Holy Spirit, and also that my son would be with me. I prayed waiting for God's hand to bring detail to this new vision.

<u>*Night Revelation*</u>*: It was not two weeks later that I had a dream about my baby girl. I was wandering to and fro trying to find the baby. I was distraught. The baby was lost. I woke up disturbed. Two more weeks passed and I had another dream which was even more disconcerting. I was in my home. I went into my baby's pink bedroom and saw a bat hanging outside the window. Upset, I ran into my bedroom and told my husband he needed to kill the bat. With that stated, we both went to sleep (a dream in a dream in the dream). In my dream I awoke to find the bat squirming through a small hole in our bedroom window. The bat then flew into the baby's bedroom and I followed. The bat then went into the baby's crib and began to eat the baby's face as I stood in shock and watched. The dream ended.*

These two dreams undoubtedly came to bring fear, despair and discouragement. The enemies hope was to disrupt the handiwork of God. But I am familiar with my accuser and his ways.

The first dream was presenting a strong thrust from the enemy that I would lose the promise of God. I would not find and move into what was ordained for me.

The second dream wanted to convince me that my husband could care less about my newly birthed gift of God. Nothing

could be further from the truth. I had asked him to kill the bat and he went to sleep? What was that? I went to sleep as well! Did I really care?? The enemy's desire was to destroy and eat away at what was brought by God while I simply stood there watching in shock. Lies! Lies! Lies!
For some, these dreams could bring disillusionment and fear. For some they might not understand. For others they could ignore and pass this off as nothing! For me, it thrust me into warfare! Why? Because I know the sign, scent and way of the accuser. I know my God and am convinced of Him and His Word.

"so shall my word be that goeth forth out of my mouth: it shall not return unto me void, but it shall accomplish that which I please, and it shall prosper in the thing whereto I sent it." (Is. 55:11, ASV)

"No weapon that is formed against thee shall prosper." (Is. 54:17, ASV)

With faith activated I am propelled into my destiny! THIS is reality!! The dream my friend gave me <u>caused a lot of attention</u> from the enemy. This surely means the plan ahead is greater than I can imagine. Yes it is true!

"Eye has not seen, nor ear heard, Nor have entered into the heart of man The things which God has prepared for those who love Him". (1 Corinthians 2:9, NKJV)

I will have my inheritance!

Trish Groblewski

This picture (dream) was painted with very dark colors, but it actually spoke a thousand words of light.

Because the Holy Spirit was involved, the darkest of "dark sayings" became a bright light that dispelled the darkness in the night.

Prophesy:

Do not allow the enemy to feed off of the new. Do not fall asleep; because, the enemy is prowling about near the portal and window of the prophetic, looking for a way in. For as the new thing - baby comes from the Holy Spirit to you, and needs to rely on you during it's nurturing and it's growth - in its crib, the enemy will try to use those who he can, in a hidden – occult way to seek out information from you about the new baby, in order to control and <u>manipulate</u> the new thing birthed.

The enemy will try to seek out information; but, know this, that the enemy does not know everything, and will try to attach itself to the new thing, searching out information by bouncing off of you and people around you certain ideas, information, and communication, in order to try to feed off of (to find out) information about the new baby – the new thing- the new birth, because the enemy can only see the façade – face of the matter - the face of the baby of which it seeks to destroy. For:

His tail drew a third of the stars of heaven and threw them to the earth. And the dragon stood before the woman who was ready to give birth, to devour her Child as soon as it was born. (Revelation 12:4, NKJV)

The enemy will try to attach itself to the new thing to take, steal, and feed off of the new thing to strengthen himself, make himself look greater than the new thing, even taking credit for the new, trying to steal the "Glory" from Jesus by trying to make others believe the new is coming from him. But the enemy is a liar. You will see the enemy in the window of your prophetic sight, and you will be awake even as you are sleeping, and know this; that, the new has already been awakened, the Son of the divine Father will be there to help, and those who have the authority to deal with this enemy at the window of your prophetic home will be there to help you.

The enemy will be exposed through the Holy Spirit. Then the picture painted by the revelation in the night will be transformed from darkness to light, for the picture spoke a thousand words of light because:

Even the darkness is not dark to You, and the night is as bright as the day. Darkness and light are alike to You. (Psalm 139:12, NAS)

(David Donnangelo)

Chapter 12

A Picture Can Speak a Thousand Words

Is a single word just simply a "word," or is there more to it? Imagine the omniscient God - Jesus, simultaneously seeing everything at the same time, all knowing of everything we know not of, knowing everyone in the past, present and the future to come in our lives, operating outside of time, knowing the past, present and future simultaneously from outside time, knowing the placement of every atom everywhere in physical creation, as well as the makeup of Heaven's light realm; able to operate in time, knowing every star, every atomic source of power release, every hair on every living being, every motive, every galaxy, every star's placement, every family from the past, present, and future, every business from the past, present, and future to come, every pastor, every person saved, every person not saved, every thought, every action, and every motive in the heart of every living being all at the same time in time, in time, as well as, outside of time, being able to be active in time and outside of time, while seeing all of it in the past, present and future in a single moment in time as we know it, without being bound to that single moment in time.

All the while, He is adjusting the earth realm and shifting things to help us all at the same time (the ebb and flow of the universe). Thousands upon thousands of miracles every second, millions of blessings poured out each hour. Knowing all, even knowing what I just mentioned at the same time I write this, and even knowing you were going to read this.

Imagine a God that awesome speaking aloud, and what the power of that a single "word' from His omniscient, omnipotent Being could have? How would that one word impact us, considering that we, in all honesty, have finite minds compared to God, and sometimes a finite imagination to even understand what He might be saying to us?

As that word comes closer and closer to us, we can only perceive its dimension on the basis of our understanding of that one "word." But the truth of the matter is, for us to "see," and understand one "word" from God, we need to understand that one "word", one picture could speak a thousand words, or even millions of words, because it came from a unlimited, omniscient, unbound God....a Holy God who directs us to the understanding of that one picture or word released and spoken.

We would have more respect for the "Word" of God if we truthfully understood all this in the concept of His omniscience. We need to have more respect when God speaks. We need to say *Holy, Holy, Holy* is the Lord God Almighty, for He spoke to us and did not have to speak to us.

Red, is a word; it is a color, an adjective. But to a "seer" it could be the Blood of Jesus, explosive power of the Dunamis of God. It could be anger expressed as rage, the color of a crayon, or the color of an apple. Yet, it is one word.

It is simply natural that the byproduct of a single "word" from God could be <u>perfumed with His omniscience</u>. After all, it came from God and it was touched by God, therefore, it could be a seed of many great things. It can literally contain an impartation of His divine supernatural "Glory" because it contains the perfume of His DNA. Holy, Holy, Holy is the Lord God Almighty.

So a single "word" from God can be a "red" hot red potato"! An explosive bomb of pure truth, and a condensed explosive Light that needs to be unpacked. Similar to the files sent to a computer that looks small, a "word" from God, but when unpacked, could contain information that requires pages of explanation of light contained in it, a light that may never go out.

Why consider a metaphor in a symbol or through a word? Because symbols can in one "word" speak an entire destiny to us when unpacked.

Like the word ROCK! Let us unpack this word. Let us look to the Bible, and to the Holy Spirit to consider what the word ROCK could mean if it was spoken by God. Here are some passages from the Bible and concepts from those passages:

Behold, I will stand before you there on the rock in Horeb; and you shall strike the rock, and water will come out of it, that the people may drink." And Moses did so in the sight of the elders of Israel (Exodus 17:6, NKJV).

"The LORD lives Blessed be my Rock! Let God be exalted, The Rock of my salvation! (2 Samuel 22:47, NKJV)

Chapter 13

Metaphor - God's Comets (Lights) from Eternity!

To me, metaphors are like God's Comets (lights) from Eternity! - The divine meteors of transformation.

A metaphor is a transferred idea, derived by a idea characterized, and echoing a type of comparison to, analogy of, or implication toward something. It is an expression (word, or phrase) that by implication suggests a similar likeness of one thing to another, and gives a recognized style to an item of speech or writing. Whether the concept consists of objects, events, ideas, activities, attributes, or almost anything expressible in communication and language, a metaphor helps make a comparison.

Metaphor in Latin means: "carrying over." In Greek, metaphor implies: "transfer," from a meaning "to carry over, to transfer." Several sources suggests it to be from "meta", meaning "between"and "phero", meaning "to bear, to carry.

From these definitions, the concept of a metaphor implies to carry an idea from one concept to another, a conceptual idea, with a like parabolic (parable) implication.

Metaphors are one of the ways the Lord speaks to us using parables. A word, a word phrase, and even unction into a certain direction through simple association are ways the Lord speaks to us. He stretches our ability to see, and He stretches our minds to perceive His vastness through making us use our minds (hearts) in ways we never thought possible.

Metaphors in dreams are God's ideas that have been touched by the omniscient mind of God, that still have a living existence and Holy fire to them, to multiply when unlocked. Simply put, if God speaks a "word," it could mean something other than what we think, or in addition to what we think, and can have unlimited potential to release revelation and dunamis that is lasting and powerful.

That the wise man may hear, and increase in learning; And that the man of understanding may attain unto sound counsels: To understand a proverb, and a figure, The words of the wise, and their dark sayings. (Proverbs 1:5-6, ASV)

It is the nature of the Lord to make us hunt for, search for, make us want to move forward to understand His ways, and at the same time, make the hunt exciting. After all, usually when we are hunting for something and the treasure is at the other end of the hunt, we want to find the treasure. The desired goal and reward of finding the understanding to what God said, however small or large in our eyes, is just waiting for us to find. It is similar to a treasure, a carrot, a pot of gold at the end of the rainbow if you will. The metaphor has a direct message, but can also have timed messages, or dimensions to unpack if spoken by God.

It is the glory of God to conceal a matter, But the glory of kings is to search out a matter (Proverbs 25:2, NKJV)

Example: Carrots and Rabbits?
What if we dreamed of a carrot being dangled in front of a rabbit?

We would expect the rabbit to want the carrot. By dangling a carrot in front of a rabbit (which is a metaphorical idea) the rabbit is quick to want the carrot, and will follow the carrot to get it wherever it goes. The carrot (end revelation) is implied to multiply fast because rabbits are fast and multiply quickly. All of this, of course, is an expression in metaphorical dynamics.

A metaphor has related ideas, or relatives in the same family such as similes, implied ideas, every day slangs implying an entirely different idea. Metaphors can be a lot of fun; and, in the fun, convey a very serious message, or a very happy message.

What if you dreamed you had ants in your pants, or you saw cats and dogs falling out of the sky, or were shown all the tea in China? What if you saw money going down a sink drain, or saw a 45 record on a record player being broken (for those who still remember record players and records)?

All these type of ideas conveyed in your dream to you could be telling you something from the Lord about yourself, or about others, that is important for you to know. The information could be valuable to you or others now, or even in the future.

Metaphors are the parables of the Lord, or condensed parables. Like a file when unzipped or unpacked, they can be filled with enormous information and also like "hot potatoes" (metaphor) of incredible information that are meant for our good, to help us move forward in our destiny, and deliver us from danger! Not to mention, of course, that sometimes the Lord simply "blows our minds" (metaphor) with what we begin to understand from a single rhema "metaphoric word" from our dream.

Metaphors are like God's comets from eternity that have residual omniscient dynamics similar to a tail on a comet. You not only see the brightness of the light of the comet as it comes closer in the night, but the makeup of the comet (the essence of the omniscient mind of God) can cause residual light that can be seen in the darkest night. The light from the tail sometimes leaves meteors that come back again, and again, and again at their own appointed hour, still displaying light in the night. It is like a timed dusting from God of His divine supernatural Glory that is holy - the golden "Glory" of His might and light.

Chapter 14

Daniel Had <u>an Excellent Spirit</u> in Him!

God can and will speak to anyone regardless of who they are, how well they live their lives, where they are, or how much integrity and good character they might have, or not have. But, there are a few clues in the Bible that will allow us to understand certain dynamics that affect the clarity and cleanness of our filters as we receive night revelation. What I mean by filters is: although we can hear from God because God simply will speak to us about something in a dream, our interpretation and perception can affect a lot of things.

If we operate without a good spirit in us, we could bring the issues we have into the interpretation of dreams. For instance, if we are bitter about an issue and bury it, forgetting it, but still allowing it to affect our life and decisions, the way we perceive a dream or other issues may not be the way God sees things.

Therefore, it is always good to look to be with people that reflect the character and mind of Jesus, and try in our lives to emulate, and learn from them how to walk in a good character, or even an excellent character like Jesus, or as Daniel did. Under his not so good circumstances, Daniel still kept his faith and integrity with God, while staying in relationship with God, and because of it, was able to live out his life with a good character.

Then this Daniel distinguished himself above the governors and satraps, because an excellent spirit was in him; and the king gave thought to setting him over the whole realm (Daniel 6:3, NKJV)

Whenever the king consulted them in any matter requiring wisdom and balanced judgment, he found them ten times more capable than any of the magicians and enchanters in his entire kingdom (Daniel 1:20, NLT)

The Bible said <u>Daniel had an excellent spirit</u>. Daniel's character and wisdom from God excelled to such a degree that he was able to live with witches, magicians, diviners, and enchanters who cast spells, and care about them. Daniel did not agree with them, but he cared about them. We in the present day as Christians sometimes forget the example of Daniel, and how Daniel was not threatened by the kind of people he was around. He knew who he was, because he feared God and was able to live out a life with a **clear conscience** because of his faith in God. He did not curse them, criticize them, hurt them, or pray against them for <u>he had an excellent spirit</u>.

Then Daniel returned to his house and explained the matter to his friends Hananiah, Mishael and Azariah. He urged them to plead for mercy from the God of heaven concerning this mystery, so that he and his friends might not be exe-

cuted with the rest of the wise men of Babylon. (Daniel 2:18, NKJV)

A good sign of a person who is walking with the Lord is that he or she can thank the Lord for what they have been given, instead of complaining about the circumstances they are in, or taking what was received from God for granted. Daniel knew that the wisdom he walked in was not because of him, but the wisdom by which he understood things came from God. Look at what the excellent Daniel says to the Lord after God revealed the King's dream to him. Daniel did not claim he was the interpreter of dreams, but he praised God for revealing the dream to him. This is a real dynamic <u>often not seen,</u> and sometimes <u>not lived out</u> by the best interpreters of dreams.

Asking the Lord, and thanking the Lord for the interpretation of dreams is something we should all do, and we should place the credit for the success of our ability to interpret dreams and revelation with God who is the interpreter of dreams.

"Blessed be the name of God forever and ever,
For wisdom and might are His.
And He changes the times and the seasons;
He removes kings and raises up kings;
He gives wisdom to the wise
And knowledge to those who have understanding.
He reveals deep and secret things;
He knows what is in the darkness,
And light dwells with Him.
I thank You and praise You,
O God of my fathers;
You have given me wisdom and might,
And have now made known to me what we asked of You,

For You have made known to us the king's demand. "
(Daniel 2:20-23, NKJV)

Daniel answered in the presence of the king, and said, "The
secret which the king has demanded, the wise men, the astrol-
ogers, the magicians, and the soothsayers cannot declare to
the king. But there is a God in heaven who reveals secrets,
and He has made known to King Nebuchadnezzar what will
be in the latter days. Your dream, and the visions of your
head upon your bed, were these (Daniel 2:27-28, NKJV).

Daniel was devoted to God, and he knew the nature
of the authority of God; and, that mysteries are revealed
by God. But, what is important about Daniel is he really
had a special, different spirit. His spirit was different -
he was so different (not like everyone else) that he was
set apart from those who had similar abilities. When he
submitted his spirit to the Rua'h hakodesh (Holy Spirit
- breath, wind, spirit of sanctity and holiness), his spirit
became empowered with a wisdom that was ten times
more than the experts of his age. His dynamic was that
of caring, humility, wisdom and understanding of the
authority of God. In other words, although he feared
God, he was not afraid to approach God on the behalf
of others. He understood authority and he acted with
a good character.

It was clear that Daniel understood that the revelations and insight into understanding his dreams and
other people's dreams did not come from him, but
came from God. Daniel also knew that dreams are sent
from God, even the dreams of those who ignore God, or
have not understood the sovereignty of the Most High.
Daniel knew which dreams were from God. Daniel
had a most excellent character. Daniel had a very dif-

ferent spirit. Daniel was set apart, and had a different and excellent spirit.

Chapter 15

"Important" Guidelines for Different Types of Dreams

In this chapter, let us examine how to understand what Jesus is really implying and saying in night revelations given to us.

And moreover, because the Preacher was wise, he still taught the people knowledge; yes, he pondered and sought out and set in order many proverbs (Ecclesiastes 12:9, NKJV)

In dreams - night revelations, we have to sometimes search the matter out. In searching the matter out, it is important we have a foundation to work from that helps us understand the dreams we have. This chapter will be of help to many, a fine tuning for some, and even shock others because they have been interpreting dreams the way they think they should, with one's own filter of understanding.

However, despite your reaction, most of this information is very well understood by people who have been helping others understand their dreams for years. There are also examples in the Bible that support this helpful information. In presenting this information, I really feel this section is one of the most important chapters to understand; it may actually give you a foundation to work from in interpreting your dreams. It will set in order, through suggestions from the information presented, many dynamics that will help you understand your dreams. If you are hungry to really understand how approach your dreams in order to understand what God is saying to you, this is the chapter for you.

It was when I first began to seek help with my dreams that Steve Bydeley (the author of the book *Dream Dreams*, along with his wife Dianne Bydeley) taught me some very important foundational principles about dreaming. It was not easy for me to accept the foundational dynamic he taught to me about dreaming, but his advice proved to be invaluable, and to this day I watch how people, even famous Christian and non-Christian people, do not get their dream interpretations totally correct.

That old joke still applies: *"When you are famous, your visions are considered important and valued; but when you are not famous, your visions are sometimes considered hallucinations and delusions."*

Only when you are a famous person, Christian prophet, or ministry leader, there is a greater responsibility to others, and the dynamics sometimes shift a little due to the boundary of authority one has. However, the <u>foundational principals</u> should still remain the same regardless.

Furthermore, there is such resistance and pride related to people who dream <u>subjectively,</u> thinking they are dreaming about others in their dream. It is a very difficult walk for leaders, interpreters, influential people, or church and family members to believe their dreams, and their interpretations might be all about them, regardless of how seemingly accurate their interpretations might appear to be. It is the real wrestling match with pride and assumption that can lead to twisted interpretations of dream revelation.

The question I always ask myself is: *"is the dreamer under some form of mentored authority? Or are they running around prophesying from their dreams and believing that which they think their dreams mean without proper advice or protective covering? Are they covered by real relational coverings that give helpful advice, or just buying (sending money or tithes) into some ministry claiming to align with them just to get the latest "buzz," the latest "high," the latest prophetic vibe, to keep their prophetic high or "fix" of prophetic intoxication going?"*

This is important, because the less covered, the less aligned with real relational communication with mentors, the more likely the enemy is going to be able to slip into ones night rest, and twist the revelations that we receive, and especially twist their interpretations through false unctions. It is also important because without proper mentoring, the more likely we are to twist the interpretation ourselves due to not thinking to have the dream tested by submitting it for an opinion to a trusted friend or mentor; and then, accepting their advice or perspective if needed.

The dreams we dream need to be determined if they are <u>about us</u>, the dreamer, or those in the dream we are dreaming about. If you have been given the office of a prophet from Jesus, your dreams may very likely <u>be about you first</u>, if you are participating in them. But, then you as the actor in your own dream (you participating), can become a symbol of the people or groups, or your family you prophesy to, or represent in the arena or boundary you have been given authority over by Jesus. A prophet can represent the "body" or church in the dream. But, as even if a famous prophet dreams subjectively, it would be wise that the prophet first look at their own life dynamic to seek revelation and accurate understanding of what they dreamed.

Prophets can represent the "remnant" in the "body of Christ," - the church that is awake to such things. All of this dynamic is subject to the boundary of authority they operate in through their real life experiences that God gave them. Not what they worked for, and not what people elected them to, but their actual appointed boundary that Jesus handed them as their boundary.

Then the prophet's dream can be associated with the boundary the prophet is operating in, be it their family, church, city, state, nation, or nations (any boundary given to a prophet by God that the person has in real life).

Simply put, it would be a real mistake to not to look at one's own life first, before venturing out to apply the interpretation of a subjective dream to others.

So, context is important. The context of the dream are the events that lead up to the night revelation in the life of the dreamer and their boundary of authority that may have triggered the dream, or are presently happening to the dreamer that the dreamer is either aware of, or is not aware of.

Subjective Dreams

This is a dream where we are participating in the dream. In this kind of dream, you are active and participating in the dream the Lord is giving you. You are active in the dream, experiencing action, emotion, and generally are interacting in the dream with others, events, or other dynamics that have you <u>participating</u> in the dream. This subjective dream experience means the dream is deliberately <u>to you</u> from the Lord. The dream is to you, for you, and <u>about you</u>, and is generally <u>not for</u>, or <u>not about</u> the people who are participating as actors in the dream with you. The dream can be related to the actors in your dream, but <u>the dream is generally to you, and for you</u> – the dream is <u>about you</u>!

By now you might be in shock, as you may of you have already presented a dream you had to someone who was participating in the dream with you, thinking you were doing them a favor, when in reality, the dream was <u>not</u> at all about them, <u>but about you</u>.

The Lord can use that other person acting in your dream to convey an aspect of their personality that is actually in you, really trying to show you what you truly, really think about that person. It can reveal what you think about a person with the same character, or what you should look at in yourself by showing you an aspect of yourself that you can see in the other individual. The person's character may be reflecting (is a mirror) of what is in your heart. That is just a small dynamic of things, just for starters, for which the other person showing up in your dream might mean.

In <u>subjective</u> divine theater, the actors in your dream that you are participating with are actors that can represent; and, can be symbolic of some aspect of the character's personality in the dream that you personally recognize, and are generally there to help you understand the meaning of what the Lord is saying to you <u>about you</u>.

Not all of these subjective dreams are symbolic either. Some dreams are literal and can be prophetic dreams, and the Lord can show you events to come.

The general rule of thumb is: if you experience anything in a dream that seems as though it could <u>not be real</u>, or could not actually happen in real life time, like flying without being in a plane, just you flying on your own, then the dream leans toward being a symbolic dream where much of the objects, people, and places could <u>all be symbolic</u> representations of something the Lord is saying to you. (Everything in the dream will lean toward being symbolic).

In general, at least 90% of every dream we all have and receive are subjective dreams <u>about us</u>. Only 10 %, if not only 5%, are objective - not about us. Most often, people who are called to operate as prophets (not just a prophetic gifting, but prophets) will be more likely to have 10% of their dreams where they are not participating in their dreams; thus, making their dream <u>objective</u> and <u>not about them</u>. Prophets generally have a greater percentage of <u>objective dreams</u> (not about them but about others) than others not operating in that calling. But most people dream dreams that are 95% about themselves, their life, and personal make up.

An example of a <u>subjective dream</u> in the Bible is found in *Genesis 28:10 – 22*. It is Jacob's Dream at Bethel. Although, in the dream Jacob sees a stairway to Heaven, God does speak to Jacob directly (a type of Theophany dream), causing Jacob to be <u>participating by hearing God</u> and <u>being directly talked to</u> by God in the dream.

Objective Dreams

These dreams are dreams that you are <u>watching</u> in the dream. You become a "seer" in the dream. You are a "watchman" watching the theater of what the Lord is showing you. Simply put, an <u>objective dream </u>is a dream where we do not participate in the dream, but watch it happening. The Lord is showing us (letting us be seers) in the night revelation and we are not at all part of it; but instead "seeing" it. (We are being shown something).

In this type of dream, what you are seeing, is not about you. (unless what you are seeing is being spoken about you, or you are seeing yourself acting something out the dream). Dreams where you see yourself acting something out have a double metaphorical implication - you are seeing yourself, and you might be seeing something going to happen to you.

So, in these objective dreams, do not place yourself in the context of the dream, or find yourself believing that you are involved in what you are seeing, except to intercede for what you are seeing, or tell the people in the dream about the dream, or tell certain trusted authority what you saw if you feel the dream is literal and not symbolic. (The dream is about what you are "seeing"). The dream is not about you!

There is a "key" to presenting this kind of dream. If you really feel the Lord wants you to tell the people who were in your dream what you saw, then you have to understand you really cannot exactly tell those who were in the dream an actual interpretation, because the dream language, dream symbols, and dream dynamics are not your own. They are not your own because, you were not participating in the dream. The dream symbols and language most likely belong to the people who you were seeing and watching in the dream. The best understanding of the symbols you saw in the dream can be interpreted by the actual people in your dream because the symbols and dream language belongs to them. And, the interpretation ultimately, as always, is

God's wisdom, because only God can ultimately give us understanding of our dreams.

A good rule about this kind of dream is to pray about telling anyone about it before you step out and tell it, and if you really feel you should tell the dream to the people who were in the dream, seek advice from a gifted dream interpreter or people placed in authority over you spiritually before you do so.

Imagine the Lord saying to you: *"Come, I want to show you something I have been aware of, and am concerned about."* Or, imagine He wants to simply share with you, and let you know about something He is aware of in order for your to pray and intercede about it. As with any friend who shares their <u>secrets</u> with you, <u>how you handle the secrets told to you</u> will most likely determine if your friend can trust you with any more secrets. He (Jesus) may not tell you any more secrets because you went and blabbed to others the details of your friend's (Jesus') secrets.

Even more revealing, you may have told the <u>secrets of someone you dreamed about</u> to others when the secrets or revelation of their character <u>was never to be revealed</u>. There is somewhat of a <u>confidentiality clause</u> to the dream stream. If you reveal what was told to you in confidence, you may not be told another thing. So, always ask the Holy Spirit if you need to tell what you dreamed to the people who you were dreaming about.

And, please remember, that if you were in any way <u>participating in the dream</u>, the dream is most likely <u>about you</u>, and not the people in your dream. The people in your dream could very well be symbolic of the general personality or character of that person, but is actually a characteristic in you, or represent someone just like the person or people in your dream.

For instance, if you like or dislike someone you dreamed about, the dreams might be revealing why you feel this way. Or people in dreams can represent someone else that you know in real life, and the person in the dream was used as a symbol the Lord gives you to represent another person. (There are real reasons why the Lord would talk in this way to you, which we discussed in the previous chapters – to code the communication and hide it from the enemy. So, you do not need to tell people what you dreamed about just because they were in your dream.

An <u>objective dream</u> is a dream <u>you are not participating in</u>, and therefore the dream is <u>not about you</u>. In this type of dream, you could be being called to intercede for what you saw. An example of two dreams that are objective in the Bible are found in Daniel 2:1 – 49.

Combination Dreams

Combination dreams are really interesting. They are dreams that directly or indirectly affect us. They involve the people, places, or events that are in the dream either symbolically, or literally. These type of dreams can indicate something coming, something that is presently happening, or something from the past that is currently affecting us, or will affect us.

The Subtleties of Combination Dreams

- ✓ <u>Subjective/Objective</u> dreams are dreams that we are at first participating in; then, as the dream progresses, we are watching what is happening.
- ✓ <u>Objective/Subjective</u> dreams are dreams that we are, at first, watching what is happening;

then, later in the dream, we become active in the dream.

Combinations can be many, and can be as simple as us being in our own house watching everything, which leans toward being a Subjective/Objective dream.

✓ Subjective/Objective dreams mean; that, we will be directly affected from what we are watching.
✓ Objective/Subjective dreams mean we will be indirectly be affected from what we are seeing in the dream.

If we are seeing something the Lord wants us to intercede for, we are likely to begin to participate in the dream after watching it (Objective/Subjective).

An example of a combination dream in the Bible is Joseph's dream found in Genesis 37:1 – 11.

Chapter 16

Literal or Symbolic? Symbolic or Literal? Or, Both Literal and Symbolic?

How can we tell the difference from a literal dream we receive, and a symbolic dream? A good rule to follow is that if our dreams have anything in them that is not something that we could do in real life, it is most likely a symbolic dream. So, if the dream just seems surreal, it is most likely symbolic throughout the whole dream.

This rule does not include Theophany, or Theophania dreams where we experience an actual appearance of God, or interact with Heaven and angels, or even dreams in which we, or others are actually being healed.

Remember, we are not of this world even though we are in it. Christians are a supernatural people (super - extra ordinary- a peculiar people living in the natural) representing Jesus and heavenly life. Therefore, we can have God, and Heaven invade our atmosphere at any time, just like when we may experience a Theophania.

Another good way we can discern if our dream is literal or symbolic is "knowing and understanding our boundary of authority."

What in real life did Jesus give us authority over? It would hardly be realistic to say we have been given authority over the White House in Washington D.C. in real life if the President is in our dream. Remember, unless you find yourself actually working in the boundary of authority as the overseer of that boundary (or working in the White House) in real life, then we cannot say it is our boundary of authority from the dream.

If the boundary in the dream seems like something not in our real life experience, the dream is most likely symbolic, and so are the people in it (There are rare exceptions to this sometimes).

This dynamic of symbolic surreal dreams, where we would not actually experience the normal in our dream, makes everything in the dream a symbol, including the people. If for instance, if we find ourselves flying in the air without getting in a plane, or flying in the air to a friend's house like a neighbor, then even the neighbor (friend) in the dream will be symbolic of someone else because we normally do not just fly without a plane.

This dream will be a symbolic dream, and the person in the dream is symbolic also, and represents someone that is like our neighbor in real life.

Remember, we sometimes are receiving encoded information from Jesus so the devil cannot know what Jesus is telling us. Jesus will sometimes use this dynamic to code the information and make us search it out. So, the less said out loud about what we dream, the less the enemy knows. Until we ask the Holy Spirit - Jesus (the author of the dream) what the symbol means, it is a good idea we keep quiet as we search the matter out, as to not allow the enemy to know what Jesus said.

Joseph had a symbolic dream in *Genesis 37:7* where he was shown his future through symbolic images of his day.

Daniel was told through a Theophany - Theophania dream he had, while having a vision (a dream while in a vision where he was shown a vision in a dream – a supernatural dream echoing revelation in Heaven) about a <u>symbolic series of events</u> echoing a literal thing that will come to pass in the end days. His spirit may not have been able to handle the burden of the revelation he was seeing. The vision was causing Daniel to tremble and become weak, so the Lord put Daniel to sleep *(Daniel 10:8 - 9)* in order to continue the vision Daniel was having (a vision while dreaming). This vision – dream was what an angel of the Lord wanted to communicate <u>through symbols</u> with him; about, what would literally come to pass in the end days.

Therefore I was left alone when I saw this great vision, and no strength remained in me; for my vigor was turned to frailty in me, and I retained no strength. Yet I heard the sound of his words; and while I heard the sound of his words I was in a deep sleep on my face, with my face to the ground. (Daniel 10: 8 – 9, NKJV)

<u>Literal dreams</u> mean that what you saw and experienced <u>can happen in real life</u>, and is <u>literal</u>, and most likely <u>should not be</u> interpreted as symbolic.

Symbolic dreams are dreams we experience that we simply would not find happening in real life, therefore the Lord is trying to tell us something with a parable-like story.

Chapter 17

Nick's Dream

Nick's Dream: I *was walking with Jesus (literally) and I could see His face which was so beautiful. We were walking together with other people (disciples). The paths we were taking were different (forests, deserts, mountains, etc…). On each path there were different obstacles, temptations, tasks, and trials that we all had to face. At each one someone was left behind because they wouldn't let go and trust Jesus. One I remember had to do with money and paying a toll to get to the next point. Another had to do with trusting the Lord that we were going the right way. All had to do with trust and required something of us.*

Finally we were climbing this steep hill and I asked the Lord if we were almost there. He replied "It's just at the top of this hill." When we reached the top, I realized that we were at this gigantic water fall that reminded me of Angel Falls. As soon as I saw the falls, I was in an inner tube raft, and the remaining people were in other rafts. Jesus smiled at us as we were heading towards the end of the falls. As I fell off I felt this rush, but also peace and I was filled with joy and woke up.

Nick's Interpretation: Since I was in the dream and inter-acting not observing, the dream was about me and for me. Jesus was showing me that although I have faced many trials He has never left my side, and I have remained with Him. He was also showing me what it takes to walk the path of righteousness with Him.

As I made it to the end of the race, as Paul called it, I believe the water fall was a metaphor for what He has for us. Seeing a waterfall is both beautiful and powerful, it repre-sents a vast amount of life giving substance that is flowing unhindered (Holy Spirit). Although I should have felt fear as I fell, instead I felt peace and joy, which I believe the Lord was trying to say is what happens when we put our trust in Him even through the toughest of times.

His lord said unto him, Well done, good and faithful servant; thou hast been faithful over a few things, I will make thee ruler over many things: enter thou into the joy of thy lord. (Mathew 25:23, NKJV)

Wow! What can we say about this dream? Awesome? Profound? What we can say is: TRUST IN THE LORD!

Nick is my best friend for many, many years. I came to know Jesus Christ personally from his friend-ship, prayers, and the prayers of his family. Nick has an anointing that seems to always echo much of what is going on in the "body" of Christ. This gift of his dream – night revelation is certainly something we can all, and should all, be able to identify with, to believe, trust, and have faith in Jesus and His Holy Spirit who cares for us.

Sometimes the Lord shows up in our dreams. However, it is not always common for Jesus to just appear in our dreams. When Jesus does show up, when Jesus appears in our dreams, there is usually a real good reason for it. And there certainly is an impartation of His "Glory" that comes to the dreamer from Jesus showing up in their dream. Although this dream was an intimate communication to Nick from Jesus between Nick and Jesus, the Lord knew, even at the time of the dream, that Nick's dream was going to end up being told in this book, and there is a profound message from Jesus in this dream. There might even be an impartation from Jesus for us in Nick's dream.

We have to thank Nick for his willingness to tell his dream. We all can identify with this dream. This dream can change lives! I hope it changes yours. If anything, I hope by reading Nick's dream, you will receive an impartation of faith, hope, and trust in Jesus.

"Blessed are the Pure in Heart for they Shall See God" *(Matthew 5:8, NKJV).*

Chapter 18

Test the Revelation!

We just read the most remarkable night revelation. It is a dream from Jesus, in fact, Jesus Himself showed up in the dream. There is no doubt about what was going on in the dream we just read. Jesus showed up! In Nick's dream, you know, that you know, that you know, that Nick was *dreaming God's dream*. In fact, you can almost feel the goodness of the dream, a goodness that is Jesus Christ and His impartation.

By this you know the Spirit of God: Every spirit that confesses that Jesus Christ has come in the flesh is of God and every spirit that does not confess that Jesus Christ has come in the flesh is not of God. And this is the spirit of the Antichrist, which you have heard was coming, and is now already in the world (1 John 4:2-3, NKJV)

Remember that the Holy Spirit – Jesus wants the best for you. Jesus may give you a dream that is a profound life-changer, possessing impartation like Nick's dream. Or, He may give you a dream like a "dark saying" to challenge you and make you feel just uncomfortable enough to wonder why you dreamed what you dreamed. Either way, Jesus only wants the best goodness for you.

Jesus sometimes speaks in dark sayings to make us look deeply into our own ways to protect us, correct, awaken, or change us, and ultimately for us to have success, love, life, peace, and wisdom in our life. In the case of Nick's dream, Jesus directly spoke to Nick, a rare occurrence to happen in which there is no doubt the dream was a dream given to Nick from God.

Dear friends, do not believe every spirit, but test the spirits to see whether they are from God, because many false prophets have gone out into the world. (1 John 4:1, NKJV)

Now we must ask ourselves if we ever test what we see, what we experience, and what we hear. But, we can do this without legalism (rules and regulations that do not allow us to believe in night revelation) and judgmental attitudes (attitudes of not believing the dreams are from God) so as to allow the possibility of believing that God does speak.

Here are some questions you can ask yourself to help you test and discern your dreams, and come to an understanding of your dream experience in the night.

- ✓ Do you feel bad or good when you wake up from the dream? How did the dream make you feel?
- ✓ Do you feel freedom, or bondage from what you dreamed? Does the dream leave you feeling tormented?
- ✓ What kind of unction are you getting from the dream you dreamed?
- ✓ Do you feel love or do you feel uncomfortable with your own conscience from the dream?

✓ Will the outcome of the dream's revelation cause you to act on it to demonstrate the "glory" of Jesus as the Lord?

✓ Does the message you dreamed make you feel inside accused or instead convicted (questioned by the Holy Spirit)?

Does the message in the dream oppose the "word" of God (the Bible)? Does it suggest to you to do anything, act a certain way, or feel about someone, events, or timed things that is not according to what you read in the Bible?

If you feel from what you were shown in the dream, that you may be living - walking things out in your life perhaps in a wrong way, or if the dream made you feel convicted of acting the wrong way, then you could be hearing from Jesus.

But ask yourself this: *"Does it feel that the Holy Spirit is suggesting to you, by showing you something through guiding you, through a personal conviction in the dream, in order to search out further your own conscience?"*

Or, does it feel like condemnation that makes you feel unable to function because you think it is God speaking but He really is not?

The devil accuses, and the Lord makes you see yourself so as to help you. Jesus does not accuse you. If you felt encouragement and a feeling of hope for your future, the dream was most likely from the Holy Spirit.

Although, there are sometimes dreams simply reflect good things that we think about in ourselves; so, in general, if your dream was an encouragement to you, giving you hope and making you feel like you have faith for the future, you are *dreaming God's dreams*.

For I know the thoughts that I think toward you, saith Jehovah, thoughts of peace, and not of evil, to give you hope in your latter end (Jeremiah 29:11, ASV)

If you feel bad about yourself, feel like you are not worth anything to the Lord or others, and if you feel you have animosity for others in what you saw, or if you feel not good about yourself from a dream you had, you may want to weigh the dream and test the message communicated. In other words, does the dream seem to be completely opposite the nature of Jesus, Holy Spirit and the Father? Always remember Jeremiah 29:11.

Ask yourself this question: *"would the Holy Spirit give me a message, and make me feel the way I do after the dream? Is the nature of the spirit communicating in the dream reflecting the character of Jesus - Holy Spirit, or the "Accuser" of the brethren?"*

Would the Holy Spirit accuse you? No! The Holy Spirit may suggest to us or convict us about something, placing on our conscience something on which to look at; but, that will not be the same as the feeling of accusation from the devil.

Then I heard a loud voice saying in heaven, "Now salvation, and strength, and the kingdom of our God, and the power of His Christ have come, for the accuser of our brethren, who accused them before our God day and night, has been cast down (Revelation 12:10, NKJV).

The devil accuses, and his goal is to make you feel bad about yourself so he can steal, twist, and kill your ability to recognize the "Glory" that is Jesus in you.

The Holy Spirit is a totally different kind of mentor. The Holy Spirit is Jesus helping us and not accusing us.

Of course, there are degrees of the Lord's communication and fire depending on our surrender to Him. Most often, authentic and accurate prophets do not get very far without hearing from the Lord, and the Lord will make sure they listen to Him. The degree the Lord may speak to a prophet who has been given authority from God can be at times filled with fire, authority, and even sometimes fearful awesomeness.

The important thing to remember is not to be so legalistic with your dreams. It is important that you recognize legalistic people who may give you interpretations, and to understand that if you are a Holy Spirit-filled Christian, then Jesus wants to give you revelation in the night. Weigh also those who will tell you that dreams are an unstable, non-reliable way to hear from God because you may be hearing from a spirit other than the Holy Spirit.

The accusative spirit of the brethren is one of the main causes we do not take our dreams seriously, justifying it with the Scripture *1 John 4:1*. However, if you read further, you will see clear <u>guidelines</u> for knowing if the spirit delivering the message is from the Holy Spirit or another spirit.

By this you know the Spirit of God: Every spirit that confesses that Jesus Christ has come in the flesh is of God and every spirit that does not confess that Jesus Christ has come in the flesh is not of God. And this is the spirit of the Antichrist, which you have heard was coming, and is now already in the world (1 John 4:2-3, NKJV)

Ultimately, it is Jesus who gives us the interpretation for dreams and night revelations.

And Pharaoh said to Joseph, "I have had a dream, and there is no one who can interpret it. But I have heard it said of you that you can understand a dream, to interpret it." So Joseph answered Pharaoh, saying, "It is not in me; God will give Pharaoh an answer of peace (Genesis 41:15 -16, NKJV).

However, when it comes to prophesy, if a dreamer delivers a message (prophesy) derived out of a night revelation, then test it by asking the dreamer if he or she believes in Jesus. If the dreamer believes Jesus is the son of God, and you ask the dreamer if he or she believes that Jesus is the only way to the salvation of one's soul, and the dreamer tells you that *"the only way to get Heaven is through Jesus,"* then you will know you can further pursue their prediction (prophesy).

Ask the dreamer if they believe other gods represented on Earth are God? The personal belief in the way prophets see the concept of God as they present their prophesies will clue you into, and help you discern the prophesies derived from their dreams. Dreams need to be interpreted correctly. The prophesies derived from prophets dreams are only as accurate as the interpretation of their dreams.

Although, God can use all sorts of ways to communicate and get revelation to us, including a donkey speaking, as seen in the Bible when Balaam's donkey spoke to him *(Numbers 22:28, NKJV)*, we do have to test what we hear and experience to see if it is from God regardless of how the Lord chooses to speak. The best interpreter of dreams and prophesy from such revelation is the Holy Spirit.

So, if you are not filled with the Holy Spirit (Jesus) and would like to be Holy Spirit-filled, go to someone who is Holy Spirit-filled and ask them to pray for you that the Holy Spirit (Jesus Christ) would fill your heart.

By this you know the Spirit of God: Every spirit that confesses that Jesus Christ has come in the flesh is of God, (1 John 4:2, NKJV)

And there are real obvious, yet sometimes controversial ramifications to what 1 John 4:3 says, which is found in the verse right after:

and every spirit that does not confess that Jesus Christ has come in the flesh is not of God. And this is the spirit of the Antichrist, which you have heard was coming, and is now already in the world (1 John 4:3, NKJV)

If you are serious about hearing from God in the night, then make sure what you dreamed is <u>written down</u>, accurately represented, truthful in what you dreamed, and interpreted correctly, even if you need help from others. Especially, when, you are about to deliver a "word" claiming to represent Jesus - Holy Spirit - God from what you dreamed.

The prophet who has a dream, let him tell a dream; And he who has My word, let him speak My word faithfully. What is the chaff to the wheat?" says the LORD (Jeremiah 23:28, NKJV)

Chapter 19

Night Revelation: Telling Our Dreams to Others

We are in a war with the enemy (the devil) even if we do not realize it. If the Lord gives you a dream that you speak out loud, you may be giving the enemy your revelation if the dream is literal or even symbolic, especially if you speak out loud your dream interpretation. Have you ever gone around telling everyone a dream that was amazing to you for no reason, or to just impress someone, only to have found yourself later in warfare over the "word" that had been given to you in the night revelation? Joseph found himself in warfare after he told his dream to his brothers (*Genesis 37, NKJV*).

So, be careful to whom, and when, and how you tell your symbolic dreams to others. The whole reason the Lord spoke to you in symbols is to prevent the enemy from understanding what He said to you. Do not give the "prince of the air" your dreams by speaking them out loud to everyone, unless you are sure you should. (If you are unctioned by the Holy Spirit to tell it.)

Point 1: Sometimes, we encounter problems with having our dreams believed and received.

And Jesus said, "To you it has been given to know the mysteries of the kingdom of God, but to the rest it is given in parables, that Seeing they may not see, And hearing they may not understand." (Luke 8:10, NKJV)

In some but not all cases, the problems in delivering revelation from our dreams are encountered at the gates of authority. Often, we do not consider how we present our dream at the gate of authority, and the truth of the matter is that it is our own fault for the problems that we encounter. We simply do not present revelation right, or do not get the interpretation right. Also, sometimes we do not catch the people in the right timing, or do not give the information with the proper spirit of respect for the individual to whom we present the dream. A good fact to remember is that wherever "true" revelation is presented, where the revelation is at the "gate," so will the enemy be also to try to stop the revelation from getting to the right people. This is also true with authority.

If the revelation is from Heaven, and not our own flesh, and it is supposed to be submitted to authority, there may be opposition from the enemy. The moment we decide to take authentic revelation to authority, the enemy will do everything to stop the revelation from getting into their hands. We might look like fools; there may be communication issues, timing issues, opposition from advisors, circumstances may happen to discredit you and the information, a delaying of the "rhema" - word from getting through; and, in turn, taking the information out of season and the timing the Lord intended.

So, be sure you are to give the revelation, and be careful because our own wrong interpretation of our dreams can cause more problems than good; because we simply do not get the interpretation or the delivery timing correct!

It is also important to note that not all the time do we need to tell leaders that the revelation we are presenting to them is from a dream that we had. Dreams may add to an already gradual download of revelation incoming from the Lord to them or you, and the night revelation may confirm or add to a better understanding of what we have been pondering to present. However, it is not always necessary to say the revelation is from a dream we had.

Sometimes, we ourselves have a know-it-all, can-do-it-all spirit. This spirit echoes our real lack of understanding that we are all on a journey of learning, regardless of the so-called level on which are reside. In night revelation or dream interpretation, this is no different. It is important to test the revelation first.

The Bible implies to: *"test revelation"* (1 John 4:1). The Bible also implies that it may be a sin not to test the revelation. So, we should realize by having a teachable spirit, and admitting we do not know everything, that it is only God that does know everything.

The point is, get your interpretation correct before venturing out to present it. Or, if you really feel you need to tell your dream, simply give the dream to those who can help you interpret it if you have a bond of trust with them, before you step out to tell your dreams to others.

Point 2: The danger of relying on one person.

In some cases, the people placed in authority over us to protect us and offer us help may not understand

127

what we are saying to them because we have not shifted to their frequency of language (understanding) to allow the same information to be translated into something practical that can be understood. The fault is our own and not the people to whom we give our revelation. Do not assume everyone speaks your language (metaphorically speaking).

No one likes to adapt a know it all, can do it all attitude; where, people are experts in every gift the Lord has given us to steward regardless if it is us, or the authority we take revelation to; but, we need to be extra sensitive and respectful at the "gate" (opportunity) with all concerned.

A know it all, can do it all attitude is a very dangerous paradigm also, because our knowledge is partial and incomplete, and even the gift of prophecy reveals only part of the whole picture! We know and prophesy in part, and we should rely on more than one person to help give a revelatory interpretation to a corporate body from the dreams we receive.

For we know in part and we prophesy in part (Corinthians 13:9, NKJV)

No one person can be expected by Jesus to do it all. That is why the Lord expects us to operate in fivefold ministry. And, no leader should expect a dreamer to tell information received in a night revelation in any another way except; what the information was, that was realized by them in the night; but, if they insist to know why the information was brought to them, and how you got it, if you are asked why you feel the Lord is speaking to you about the matter you present, after you have searched the matter out with the Lord - Holy Spirit, then you can tell authority your dream.

Point 3: *Absolute authority corrupts absolutely ... The Pied Piper syndrome.*
(Don't be following the absolute pipers and the tune coming from their pipes.)

Absolute authority corrupts absolutely because it is usually unchecked, not accountable to any other authority, and even ultimately not accountable to itself.

There are many in the body of Christ that are followers (groupies of "celebrity" of the next big thing to comes along) looking to have their own 15 minutes of fame.

Unfortunately, sometimes the pipers that the mice are following are not exactly looking out for the flock, sometimes they are looking out for their own families or lifestyles, even sometimes they are looking for more prosperity to fuel the financial freedom of their ministries in the Kingdom as the true motive that is in their heart. All the while hoping, through the desire driven ministry and the pursuit of their financial freedom, they will be able to touch someone with the Holy Spirit. Although, most all churches and ministries, or even sometimes businesses, never originally start out looking to make a buck, or operating their churches and ministries like a business without first serving others, sometimes the demands of the world slowly take over, and the dynamic in ministry shifts from trust in God for provision, to business as usual. Often times, in this shift, the ministries begin looking to collect the spoils of ministry without serving others first, and this can lead to all sorts of absolutes that get hidden in the mix of what is really going on.

The tunes from those kinds of pipes of need and greed, and unaccountable celebrity are the wrong tunes that can take one off the path of one's own destiny, or manipulate the dynamics of one's future by trying to coral the body of Christ to follow a given ideal, when Jesus is really not doing any of it. The tune will be an absolute tune that sounds like: if you don't do this, that will happen; or, if you don't do that, this will happen.

You do know what happened to the mice that followed the piper's tune, don't you?

So, when you deliver your revelation from the dreams you have to authority; do not go in like you yourself are an authority either, just because you received the revelation from God. Be polite and humble, and seek a common ground of communication to deliver your revelation so you can discuss it without absolutes. In fact, if you interpret your dreams, or others interpret your dreams in the same manner of the absolute piper, where this symbol means this, and that symbol means that, and could not possibly mean anything else, it could lead you to the end of a cliff where there is no were to go except down. ✄

[The absolute idea that the authorities placed over us to protect us have the same gifts; and, operate in them better, has to be weighed and tested. If that ✗ were true, I could simply hand a paint brush to those placed in authority over me and ask them to produce a photo realistic painting in a given time frame, and expect them to do it just like me but better. The question also would be: "what will they paint"? What will actually be painted, and what is the fruit of looking at the painting?]

That is not to say, that the opinions from leaders should be ignored either, as usually the unction of the Holy Spirit is operating in those we would need to take a dream revelation to, and they can certainly weigh the revelation in a helpful manner. Authority is there to suggest application, to protect us, to seek the best understanding in applying and directing us in our destiny and ideas, and help keep us in line with Biblical principles, to look after us in our walk of faith, to help us act and live in the character of Christ. Authority is placed in our lives by Jesus to protect us and help us develop a fulfilling relationship with Him (Jesus Christ) first and foremost.

We all are (including leadership) actually sent to authority to help them, they intern are supposed to be protecting us. If we receive a dream and we feel we need to present the dream to those the Lord has placed in authority over us, we need to get it right. Have the correct interpretation before you take a corporate revelation to your leaders. Don't waste their time. And, do not go in with an attitude of absolute authority that you have the only interpretation and answer for them.

And, be aware that Leaders may sometimes receive so many dreams, so many revelations, or so many dreams presented to them in a way that the presenter thinks that the Leader doesn't have a clue to such profound information: that, sometimes leaders simply have had enough! They get revelation burn out from the revelators. This is especially scary if all the so called revelations presented are not for the corporate body at all, but personal revelations meant for the dreamer, or prophetic receiver.

Here is something that will be very helpful to you. Keep in mind that our boundary of authority given to us by the Lord can affect the meaning off the night revelation the Lord sends us, and not every dream is supposed to be handed over to authorities, even if those authorities are actually in our dreams.

So, be polite, careful, and respectful to those you discuss your revelations with, and present your revelations with the idea of God's unlimited possibility instead of Satan's absolutes.✗✗✗

Point 4: What is the Fruit of the Dream?

Leaders don't usually think they are responsible to be the only people who dream and hear from God, and can interpret your dreams, or revelations. Good leadership most often has more than a few people who can discern what you present by praying it through with the Holy Spirit.

The prophet who has a dream, let him tell a dream; And he who has My word, let him speak My word faithfully. What is the chaff to the wheat?" says the LORD (Jeremiah 23:28, NKJV).

This passage clearly shows that dreams are subject to evaluation, and can be words from the Lord, or can be the fabrications of the flesh of the individuals dreaming. In either case, "what does straw have to do with grain"? Grain is food and a seed; whereas straw can be used to burn, or build with, and a host of all sorts of things. But, the grain is fruit. So, we must ask ourselves: "what is the fruit of the dream"? Is what we are presenting going to be used to build with, start a revival fire with, burned to get rid of it, or weaved to make a basket and other valuable things out of it? Or, will what we present be a seed the produces growth and more seeds and fruit for the future. In other words, one had better have the correct interpretation to give, or be honest enough to say they do not understand what the Lord is saying if they give it.

So, we all should be careful, to whom, and when, why, and how we tell our dreams to others by asking God for wisdom. Also, we can be polite and humble in our approach to delivering dream revelation when we feel we should share what we have dreamed.

Chapter 20

Your Boundary of Authority

In most cases, when we dream and receive revelation, even if we are dreaming about other places in the world, or famous people, or unique miracles, the settings for our dreams and the context of our present day situation is very important. God has given each of us a boundary of authority, a sphere of authority, a garden to maintain just like Adam and Eve received. We have to understand that although our dreams can be remarkable, our boundary of authority with regard to them should be dictated by God. That is why the context of our dreams and the context of our real everyday lives are important.

If you are a pastor, you may dream about things in your boundary of authority related to events, people, and future happenings in your church. If you are a family-loving person who is working at home, your dreams could very well be related to your family and home. If you are an intercessor, the Lord may tell you who and what to pray for in a dream. If you are placed in a territory overseeing it as a watchman for the Lord, (such as a city, county, state, nation, or representative for a ministry, government agency, or church), you most likely have a boundary of appointed authority from the Lord for that, and your dreams may very well be echoing things, events, and revelation received as strategy for your appointed boundary.

The important thing to remember is to stay in your boundary.

Boundaries are actually created by the Lord to keep us safe, just as Adam and Eve first were given a boundary in the garden of Eden. But, when they ventured outside their appointed boundary and chose to not stay in their designated place (not obeying the rules set in place in that given boundary), they lost their appointed boundary. They realized they were vulnerable because they did not trust the Lord like a child trusts their parents, and it made them vulnerable even to themselves. Their innocence and trust in the Lord kept them protected.

Their childlike faith kept them protected until they chose to not have faith and not believe the Lord; that is, to not partake of certain things the Lord told them not to, as it would not be in their best interest. We all have Adam and Eve's DNA in us, and in our human nature we do things we are told not to do just out of curiosity. When we venture into an area where we were not given permission to be in, we may not be protected, and it could result in loss, or even worse - rejection into paradise.

So the question is: *"Is our boundary of authority from God in our own house, or other houses, or even perhaps outhouses?"*

Ask yourself this question: *"Am I an <u>outhouse</u> prophet or an <u>in-house</u> prophetic dreamer? Am I a dreamer under the authority of a house, protected by a house, or am I a dreamer*

*that lets anything have access to me because I dream out-
side the boundary of a covering or advice, uncovered without
a roof, or even outside the boundary of the fellowship of
authority who know me and are protecting me?"*

If you are a stranger to those you think you should
give your dream revelation to, you may find yourself
in an odd and peculiar dynamic. Although, Jesus can
give us revelation in the night that is for others we
do not know, it is not usual for the Lord to send us to
people we do not know; even though, it could happen
that the Lord may choose to. If it does happen that you
receive a revelation you are told to deliver to people
you do not know, and who do not know you, will you
deliver it as an outhouse prophet; or, or will you get to
know the people first, and deliver your revelation as
an in-house prophet?

Are you an outhouse prophet or an in-house
prophet? In other words, do you know the people you
are bringing your revelation to? Do they know you? In
all the knowing, be aware of this: No house, ministry,
business or pastor is in any way obligated to act on
your night revelation whether they know you or not.

This is important to grasp right away, especially if
you are from one place (area), and enter another place
(territory). You should take your revelations to the City
Elders, Church Elders, Apostolic Leaders, or those in
authority in the place you feel you were sent to tell
your night revelation first. Do this in order to work
with them, so they can help you work through your
concerns.

The term **outhouse** originally was used to describe
and referred to an **outside building**, or a house, or any
small structure away from a main building, used for a
variety of purposes, but mainly for things and activities

not really wanted in the area of the main house. Later, it was associated with a place away from the main house that one goes to relieve themselves of unwanted waste. I am writing this to help us understand the metaphorical significance of this.

We need to understand that some will receive us when we need to tell them a dream, and some will not care. But, if we are honest with ourselves and operate politely, delivering the revelation from the dream with respect, our delivering of the dream is the best we can do. Once we deliver the information, and politely are able to discuss our thoughts with leaders in charge, we must understand that we have walked out what we were supposed to do.

If you expect anything beyond that, you may get hurt because you were trying to operate beyond your boundary of authority, and as a result, you may end up with a hurt spirit or a bitter root that could grow into a very bitter root that the enemy will use to gain access to you.

Before you take your revelation to authority, ask yourself: *"what is my "true" motive for giving the night revelation to authority?"* Do you really have to tell anyone your night revelation? Before you make a mountain out of a mole hill, consider that you may end up making a fool out of yourself by making something look bigger than what it really is, and as a result, get buried under a mountain from an avalanche of reactions that were on the mountain.

"I have heard what the prophets have said who prophesy lies in My name, saying, 'I have dreamed, I have dreamed! How long will this be in the heart of the prophets who prophesy lies? Indeed they are prophets of the deceit of their own heart, who try to make My people forget My name by their dreams

which everyone tells his neighbor, as their fathers forgot My name for Baal. The prophet who has a dream, let him tell a dream; And he who has My word, let him speak My word faithfully. What is the chaff to the wheat?" says the LORD. Is not My word like a fire?" says the LORD, " And like a hammer that breaks the rock in pieces? (Jeremiah 23:25 -29, NKJV)

If you do decide to step out and reveal the dream you think is for the "body" of Christ, be aware that the people you give your dream to simply may not be interested in your dream. As Barbara Wentroble from International Breakthrough Ministries always teaches, SW,SW,SW is the advice we should live by and walk in if we must deliver revelation. "Some will," "Some won't," "So what!" If you expect anything beyond that, you may be venturing outside your boundary of authority, into a boundary not meant for you.

If the revelation given to you is used by the Lord as a hammer to break through, then so be it - it becomes a hammer! All you need to know is; that, you were faithful in delivering the information.

Chapter 21

Why Can We Not Remember Our Dreams?

For God may speak in one way, or in another, Yet man does not perceive it (Job 33:14, NKJV).

Here are some reasons, metaphorical as well as natural, why we can't remember the dreams we have had:

1) Do we really believe Jesus can talk to us in our dreams, and do we take our dreams seriously enough to pay attention to them? Do we consider our dreams to be holy or "Holy" - ordinary, and common, or extraordinary and priceless?

For whoever has, to him more will be given, and he will have abundance; but whoever does not have, even what he has will be taken away from him. (Matthew 13:12, NKJV)

There is a rather convicting metaphorical statement of the truth here about dream revelation in the night. To those who listen to their dreams, more understanding, and more dreams will be given to fulfill their dreams. But those who ignore their dreams, will have less dreams to dream, and if they still do not get the hint, the dreams they do have will be taken away.

Listen to what the Bible further says:

And in them the prophecy of Isaiah is fulfilled, which says: 'Hearing you will hear and shall not understand, And seeing you will see and not perceive; (Matthew 13:14, NKJV)

For the hearts of this people have grown dull. Their ears are hard of hearing, And their eyes they have closed, Lest they should see with their eyes and hear with their ears, Lest they should understand with their hearts and turn, So that I should heal them (Matthew 13:15, NKJV).

But blessed are your eyes for they see, and your ears for they hear; (Matthew 13:16, NKJV)

for assuredly, I say to you that many prophets and righteous men desired to see what you see, and did not see it, and to hear what you hear, and did not hear it. (Matthew 13:17, NKJV)

Now, we must ask ourselves if we have been rebellious to God (Jesus). Have we laughed at the idea that our dreams can be significant? Do we laugh at others who dream, calling them dreamers and mock them, or think our way of receiving revelation from Jesus is better than the dreamer who dreams dreams? All revelation from Jesus in Heaven is for our benefit.

If we simply do not take dreams seriously (either in the way we view dreams, or the way we do not value them) then this can be one of the reasons we do not receive night revelations. If we have really realized what we have been missing in not believing our dreams, or taking them for granted, or mocking dreams or the dreamer, then there is something we can do. One of my favorite sayings of redemption in the world is from Dr. Robert Heidler from Glory of Zion in Denton, Texas. He has a great suggestion for us to walk out. He says: *"I have good news for you, you can repent!"* This means you can change your thinking (turn around) from not believing and believe. It is that simple!

"Son of man, you dwell in the midst of a rebellious house, which has eyes to see but does not see, and ears to hear but does not hear; for they are a rebellious house (Ezekiel 12:2, NKJV).

God will conceal the truth from those who refuse to believe *(Matthew 13:12, NKJV).* Jesus wants us to search out the answer to His parables.

When you give revelations of God to those who do not believe, it simply increases their opposition and condemnation. Similarly, if Jesus gives us a revelation in the night, and we do not pay attention, do not take it seriously, and do not believe He is speaking, we are likely not to receive another revelation in the night, until we repent or change our minds and hearts about the way the Lord is choosing to speak to us.

"Do not give what is holy to the dogs; nor cast your pearls before swine, lest they trample them under their feet, and turn and tear you in pieces (Matthew 7:6, HKJV).

Do not let people take something valuable from Heaven like <u>dream revelation,</u> and make it common and unimportant to the point of it being useless. Do not let that which is Holy, be defiled, and defined as common and generic to the point of it becoming trampled on.

To explicate a contrast of what is ordinary and common, or taken for granted, or often times not taken seriously enough to be believe as holy, with that of "Holy" and unique and deserving of a King or Queen, I expressed deliberately throughout this book word illustrations of what is holy and "Holy", what is the glory, and what it "Glory" - deserving of capitalization – and a special treatment because it is of God.

God gives us the privilege to be part of what is "Holy" (treats us with integrity as "Holy", and gives us an opportunity to discover the glory in us as "Holy"- his "Glory" in us). God lets us search the matter out and see His Kingdom of God through His parables because it is a privilege to do so.

That which is "Holy" unto God is in a class all its own. We sometimes make that which is "Holy"(reflecting the eternal awesome "Glory" of God) a common holy and glory. There is holy, and then there is "Holy"- that which reflects God's eternity and "Glory"! God treats us "Holy" with the same integrity, as if we are Kings and Queens, and have the wisdom like King Solomon, that is if we respect His ways and His dreams. In some ways, we are only as holy as our recognition and respect of the "Holy" uniqueness of our awesome God – the wholeness and uniqueness of the "Glory"of God.

It is the glory of God to conceal a matter, But the glory of kings is to search out a matter. (Proverbs 25:2)

Therefore I speak to them in parables, because seeing they do not see, and hearing they do not hear, nor do they understand (Matthew 13:13, NKJV).

142

God's mysteries are for those who take Him seriously; regardless of the way God chooses to speak to us. Dr. Chuck Pierce, President of Global Spheres, and Glory of Zion Ministries in Denton, Texas, is honestly one of the most gifted dream interpreters I have ever encountered. I think this is primarily because he has the "word" of God in him from studying the Bible. As I have mentioned before, he has often said: *"Dreams that have not been interpreted, are like letters sent to you that have not been opened."* I think this statement has <u>great depth</u> of meaning, and an unlimited application, if we can really grasp the dimension of what was said about dreams here.

So, take your dreams seriously and open the letters, and experience the profound dimension of the dream. They are the dreams you dream, that could be God's dream for you that can make you realize your dreams as you live His dreams.

2) We simply did not pay attention to what Jesus said in the last night revelation he gave us! To pay attention is not enough though, we must act on the revelation - do exactly what he wanted us to do, look at exactly what He was showing us, pray for whom He wanted us to pray for, etc…

We must obey Jesus and what he showed us in last dream we had.

If we are not receiving night revelation from Jesus, then He may be waiting for us to pay attention to the last thing He told us to do.

3) We have grieved the Holy Spirit. In this instance, we are living in the flesh, and not operating with our hearts fixed on the Lord. We have been duped by the

rituals, formulas, and religion of men, instead of being led by the Holy Spirit.

There are many ways that we can grieve the Holy Spirit and chase away the angels. Living in sin, of course, is the most obvious way. So we really want to be in good relationship with Jesus - the Holy Spirit in order for more revelation to come to us. We should try to live good and honest lives.

One of the most common examples explaining how we can grieve the Holy Spirit is the analogy of a bride and groom, or even business partner. If your wife or husband suddenly stops talking to you, if your business partner suddenly stops speaking to you, what does that usually mean? If the bride groom is not talking to the bride, the bride had better find out what is bothering the groom. If your business partner stops talking to you, your business may not move forward smoothly, and you may need to take inventory, or may need to re-examine your relationship before a breach in "trust" might occur. Someone had better take a good inventory as to what is happening around them if this happens, and watch how, and ask why they are acting the way they are acting, and wonder what they are doing themselves that might be causing the lack of communication.

Usually when the groom, husband, business partner, or wife stops talking to the partner, or spouse, someone is grieved about something.

What we should consider is this: Is the Holy Spirit grieved? Is the Holy Spirit - Jesus troubled about the last time you had a conversation together? And, if so, why? I bet your spouse or your friend can get your attention if they stop talking to you! Don't let Jesus get your attention in the same way!

To those who listen to my teaching, more understanding will be given, and they will have an abundance of knowledge. But for those who are not listening, even what little understanding they have will be taken away from them. (Matthew 13:12, NLT)

4) God seals the dream. Sealed dreams cannot be remembered because God seals them, preventing us from remembering them, until the time we should, and the necessary preparation is developed in our lives and others lives for the revelation to come forth, often times to protect us, including protecting us from ourselves and our own pride.

In order to turn man from his deed, And conceal pride from man, (Job 33: 17, NKJV)

Sometimes the Lord gives us a lot of information that can be profound, so profound that we may be tempted to tell others or think of ourselves better than we should. So God seals the revelations so we cannot remember them, thus preventing us from becoming prideful, or being set up for a fall from curses of envy. This can also protect us from ill wishes from people who perceive pride in us. Pride comes before the fall!

Pride goes before destruction, and a haughty spirit before a fall. (Proverbs 16:18, NKJV)

Then, if and when the Lord does break the seal, all of a sudden we remember the dream we had. While hearing, experiencing, or understanding what is going on in a flash of illumination (light), we realize we have somehow seen what we are experiencing before. As we walk through the experience, our past dream is recalled and remembered in a flash of illumination. We sometimes refer to the experience as a déjà vu (already been seen) experience. The revelation of remembering comes with such light that the experience can have an effect on us from simply remembering it. It is a deep experience of the flash of remembering with light, of a second in time having a strong depth to it, to the point of almost having a mysterious quality to it, or sometimes having an anointing to it.

If Jesus seals a dream, He could be giving us wisdom to walk out our life, only our conscious mind cannot remember it because He sealed it. However, the information is in our subconscious, giving us wisdom in our daily lives. If we do have a déjà vu experience, then the Lord has broken a seal in our minds! And, the Lord wants us to know He broke the seal. Why would he want us to know that He broke the seal? Possibly, the Lord is telling us that He is about to astound us with wonder, and astound the people who are involved in the remembered thoughts from the previous dream. The dream that we had from the Lord is about to become a revelation of wonder.

Perhaps Jesus is telling us to remember Him, as who He is in all of it, and to watch for His astounding signs and wonders involved.

Therefore once more I will astound these people with wonder upon wonder; the wisdom of the wise will perish, the intelligence of the intelligent will vanish." (Isaiah 29: 8 -14, NKJV)

So, do not be worried about not remembering your dreams, but instead, be faithful and prayerful the Lord will let you dream His Dreams.

Chapter 22

What to Do When We Have a Dream and Want It To Come True?

The first thing we have to do to make our dreams come true is to **"Wake Up"**, <u>write the dream down</u>, and begin to pray about the dream. <u>Write the vision down</u>. Let me repeat, when you have a dream, do not be afraid of <u>writing it down</u>. Often when we write the vision down, we can actually get further revelation on what we dreamed about, and sometimes the dream is revealed to us by simply <u>writing it down</u>.

Then the LORD answered me and said: " Write the vision And make it plain on tablets, That he may run who reads it. (Habakkuk 2:2, NKJV)

In the Bible, Habakkuk shows us to write the vision down, so that the vision can come to pass by running with it. Jesus sometimes will give us destiny revelations to give us a hope for the future, and as the appointed time comes for the prophesy of what the Lord spoke to us in the night comes close, the revelation gains momentum to defeat obstacles from the enemy that may try to stop the "word" over our lives from happening. But, we must be good stewards of the "word," wise stewards, and obey the timing of the Lord.

Often, when we have an incredible revelation from the Lord about our destiny, we are excited to share what the Lord has told us, and what the Lord Himself is celebrating in us because He created us to fulfill our destiny in Him and become whole. But, as we begin to share our dreams with others, **run with the dream**, some people may not be on the same page. Perhaps they are experiencing issues in their own lives, or simply may not be on your side. There is wisdom to be careful if the Lord has given you a destiny dream where you may feel something incredible might happen to you. Even though the vision of what the Lord told you will come to pass at the Lord's appointed hour, it is important that we understand that we do have to act, walk out, prepare, get trained, and be aligned to move forward with it. We also have a responsibility not to act presumptuously, tell the wrong person, or simply get puffed up with a false self-confidence and pride. We need to keep ourselves in check so that the vision - night revelation will not be delayed moving into the appointed time.

When Joseph told one of his dreams to his brothers, his brothers did not exactly support him (metaphorical). In fact, they first intended to kill him, but then got rid of him by selling him into slavery. Similarly, some of our own brothers and sisters in Christ, or even those close to us who we have known for years, may not react to our dreams with excitement and blessing. They may instead have an entirely different reaction.

So, having wisdom, understanding, trusting the Lord (Holy Spirit), and having proper discernment is necessary to allow the night revelations to mature, and for us to get aligned with the Lord and His purposes shown to us in the dreams. *God will put His finger on an appointed time when all the dynamics of what was revealed in the dream will come together and the appointed time is ready to happen.*

For the vision is yet for an appointed time; But at the end it will speak, and it will not lie. Though it tarries, wait for it; Because it will surely come, It will not tarry. (Habakkuk 2:3, NKJV)

After you journal a dream (write the vision down), and you have pondered it over with the Holy Spirit (Jesus), if you feel you want to share your dream, find someone you can trust. Find someone who likes you, and do not be fooled into just giving your dream to a person just because they are followers of Jesus or people with whom you are acquainted. Instead, use wisdom; and, if you really feel to share your dreams, give your dreams to someone who supports you, loves you, who likes to run with you, and most importantly, make sure you do not give your dream to someone who is will be jealous of what the Lord speaks to you. You would be very surprised how that spirit of jealousy can manifest when you tell your dreams.

"And his brothers said to him, "Shall you indeed reign over us? Or shall you indeed have dominion over us?" So they hated him even more for his dreams and for his words (Genesis 37:8 KJV).

🕐 *So, the first thing you have to do to have your dreams come true is to "Wake Up" to the possibility of it being something new!*

🕐 Then, the second thing we should do is <u>write the dream</u> (night vision) <u>down</u> so that it becomes recorded as a permanent word from the Lord.

🕐 For it speaks of the end result and will not prove false, it tells us what dream God has for us, it tells us God's dreams for us. It suggests how to get to the end result which is always to help us, to deliver us from our own issues, and to bring us to the fullness, goodness, and "Shalom" of Jesus. It will not be proven false because God is the author of the vision for your life.

🕐 Of course, that means we need to be aware that not every idea and vision we personally have for our lives is what God wants for us. So, we should always be trying to align with God's will for our lives, and what better way to be spoken to, than in the night by the Holy Spirit (Jesus).

Chapter 23

Blessed are The Pure in Heart
for They Shall See God!
(Matthew 5:8, NKJV).

"Blessed are the Pure in Heart for they Shall See God (Matthew 5:8, NKJV)."

There are all sorts of dreams and all kinds of ways the Lord can speak to us through night revelation. In most all cases, the dreams we receive from the Lord are to help us, our families, friends, churches, our society, cities, states and nations.

The Lord wants to bless us in the night, but sometimes the Lord weighs whether to give profound revelation to those who have a mocking spirit that defiles His purposes. This defilement comes through mocking dreams and such possibility of revelation from Heaven. In reality, mocking God's dreams given to help us in our lives <u>opposes the will of God </u>by exalting one's intelligence above the Creator of all that is known, and all that cannot be comprehended.

God will give those with a childlike heart revelation because, as the Scripture says, "people with a pure heart are blessed and they shall see God" *(Mathew 5: 3-10)*. To God, the heart of a child is innocent before being influenced by that which is not beautiful. So, to God, it is beautiful to wait in hope and innocence with a pure heart for Him to speak in the night.

It was once attributed that Saint Gregory of Nyssa had said: *"a beatitude is a possession of all things held to be good, from which nothing is absent that a good desire may want."*

Dreams can be beautiful ... dreams can give us direction ... dreams can tell us what we do not see ... dreams can that tell us what is really in our hearts.

With all that stated, I wanted to share with you a dream that Pastor Jack Groblewski has allowed me to present. Pastor Jack is the senior Pastor of NC4 (New Covenant Christian Community) in Bethlehem, Pennsylvania, and Apostolic Council to the "Grace Network" of Churches in Pennsylvania and Virginia. This dream simply "is" a "beatitude."- *"a possession of all things held to be good, from which nothing is absent that a good desire may want."*

It is a remarkable dream meant to encourage us, most likely even to encourage Pastor Jack. It encourages the "body of Christ, and perhaps hints to a covenantal walk of "Grace" that can cause the light of Christ to illuminate every step of the way. I have a really unique feeling about this dream, that it possibly has revelation in it that has not yet been discovered.

As with all the dreams presented in this book, the Lord knew that this dream would be presented to help us to build our faith. It is clear from this night revelation that, the Lord has a "new dimension" to introduce in His plan for His church. (Because of the boundary of Pastor Jack's authority given to him by Jesus, this dream has implications for the entire "body" of believers in Christ Jesus).

Pastor Jack's Dream: *I dreamt that I was in a room with three side walls, a floor and a ceiling. On one wall was a blackboard with a diagram on it. As I was standing in the room, I realized that Jesus was there. He hadn't appeared. He had been there and it was as if I simply became conscious of His presence. I don't ever remember actually seeing Jesus in a dream before this or since. The most surprising thing about Him was how "normal" he looked and acted, and how strikingly friendly he was. I know that the idea of Jesus as simply friendly seems a bit cheeky. I've always felt that... "friendship with Jesus" kinds of teachings... undermined Jesus' divinity. But, there was this incredible sense of his friendliness and there was an easy grandeur about it. He pointed toward the open side of the room and said, "Tell them to go in my name and tell them I am present." As I looked out of the room through the open side I saw a gorgeous horizon, some slight red but primarily golds and whites. Suddenly I was in complete darkness but as I lifted my foot to take a step everything became light again and the light was sustained as I kept moving. As I reached the edge of the room and looked down I was walking on a floor that was radiating different colors, rather like the aurora borealis.*

As I looked down the voice said, "This is the name of the Lord." I awoke from a deep sleep and knew this was from God. The Sunday following I gave an exhortation to the church to "Go or move forward in the name of the Lord. His presence is here and with you."

My limited interpretation is as follows: *The diagram on the blackboard is a picture of a new dimension of His plan for both me and the church. It is on a blackboard because He is going to school me in it. The room is a room of education and revelation. It is open-ended because the outside is the place of the application of what He purposes to do. I'm not sure about the colors of the horizon though I sense that the red signifies a storminess or opposition of some kind, but the richness of the gold and whites suffusing the red suggest to me that his divinity and holiness will overcome whatever rough weather may lie in store. The light going out and then coming on as I moved means that as we walk in a progression of obedience, it will sustain our light. The changing colors of the floor represent the names of God and titles of God throughout scripture. As we move forward, the different names of God that reveal different aspects of God's character will be revealed to us at key moments as we need to appropriate them. I don't know what to make of the predominant friendliness except to simply say how enjoyable Jesus is.*

I found it interesting that Pastor Jack had given me this dream right on the anniversary date of the largest recorded geomagnetic storm that ever occurred, where the Aurorae was seen around the world, and were the Aurorae was so bright that, their glow awoke gold miners, who began preparing breakfast because they thought it was the morning and time to wake up.

And so we have the prophetic word confirmed, which you do well to heed as a light that shines in a dark place, until the day dawns and the morning star rises in your hearts (2 Peter 1:19, NKJV)

Dreams can be so filled with the presence of Jesus and Heaven that they become markers of eternity, a guidepost of revelation to the new. This new plan of Jesus seems to include a foundational walk of covenantal illumination (covenantal revelation – a relational revelation – a revelation of relationships).

This illumination is grounded in the dunamis of the most Holy of Names of the God:

~ **Elohim** - our Creator;
~ **Jehovah** - our Lord God;
~ **El Shaddai** - our Supplier;
~ **Adonai** - our Master;
~ **Jehovah Jireh** - our Provider,
~ **Jehovah Rophe** - our Healer;
~ **Jehovah Nissi** – our Banner;
~ **Jehovah Mikkadesh** – our Sanctifier;
~ **Jehovah Tsidkenu** – our Righteousness;
~ **Jehovah Shalom** – our Peace, Fullness, Prosperity, Well Being, Happiness and Joy;
~ **Jehovah Rohi** – our Shephard; and
~ **Jehovah Shammah** – His Abiding Presence!

Jesus' new plans in this dream shown to Pastor Jack seem to imply for us to understand the most Holy names of the Father and their meaning as a foundation of covenant in "faith" and revelation. It certainly can encourage us to go forth and move forward in the name of the Lord. As Pastor Jack suggests: *"His presence is here with us now."* We all can walk in covenant with each other like the Pastor was shown by Jesus that he does.

Prophesy:

Look for the removing of the walls in the places where we learn, and even the walls in what we have learned in that which is called church. As one of the four walls is removed from the place that is containing My wisdom, when one of the four walls that is blocking the view is removed, the opening will become a door to a new dimension - the dimen-

155

sion of creative possibilities for you to see the horizon line of the future before it becomes now. For, just as at high altitudes there is a freedom to "be," and My oxygen red dominates, there will be a returning of that freedom to "be" and the ability to breath even to a ground level from an excited state; where, you will be able to move, and catch the wind of My Son. For as this comes to pass, creation shall be excited by the collision of my Son's wind (Holy Spirit) with them, there will even be an excitement as My freedom returns to a grounded state, for I will show you there is no limit to the dimension of "Glory" that can manifest in your walk of covenant as you "Go," and as your walk of "Covenant" decrees My Names across the earth.

(David Donnangelo)

Chapter 24

God Can Answer Your Questions in a Dream?

Call unto me, and I will answer thee, and will show thee great things, and difficult, which thou knowest not. (Jeremiah 33:3, ASV)

Dreams can be beatitudes … dreams can heal … dreams can protect us and warn us … dreams can give us direction … dreams can invade our space … dreams can tell us what we do not see … dreams can that tell us what is really in our hearts … dreams can reveal what is really in the hearts of others, even people we do not know … dreams can reveal the truth … dreams can literally impart the anointing of the Lord for a specific purpose the Lord has in mind … dreams can impart wisdom … dreams can give us inventions like the sowing machine, or even formulas like the theory of relativity, or structures of chemicals like benzene. For those of you who prefer to be golfing rather than taking seriously your dreams, you could perhaps find a new way to hold your golf club in a dream. Yes, you can enjoy your golf game and believe in your dreams all at the same time.

Dreams can give us a song, or a "sound" that can change our lives and the lives of others. Dreams can answer the questions of our hearts, and give us new plans, or glimpses of new plans for the future.

I remember when I asked the Lord about continuing to go to the Issachar School founded by Dr. Robert Heidler and Dr. Chuck Pierce. I had already completed the three years planned for the school, but the dynamic seemed to shift a bit and continue with extended programs of education at the Issachar School. So, I was pondering the Issachar School, and why I would continue in it. Most specifically, I was pondering if I should continue taking courses offered at the Issachar School as it had already evolved from the point of first opening to the completion of the three years.

It was not too hard to decide to continue going to the Issachar School, but the Lord decided to step in, and make His own statement about the School. Only when the Lord answers one of your questions, you could be left with your mind totally blown, revelation hitting you in every direction, and even experiencing a glimpse of the Lord's unlimited potential to do anything. I simply was pondering through questions, and got an answer in a night revelation. I receive an answer from God that was rather dramatically convincing in a way only God can do it.

The response to just my thoughts through a night revelation was direct and unbelievable. God decided to weigh in on my discussions, and express His heart in the matter. It was an amazing, unbelievable, and incredible – an out of this world dream. There was simply no way my mind could have even invented what I dreamed, or experienced what happened to me as a result of simply pondering the Issachar School.

Night Revelation (Dream):

I found myself sitting in an Issachar class in which, Dr. Robert Heidler was teaching us about the "Word" of God, and using blueprints and PowerPoint notes through charts to teach us. Only, the blueprints in the charts he was using were blueprints to the Temple of Israel in Jerusalem, and at the same time, as Dr. Heidler was teaching with the blueprint charts, the charts were also the blueprints for the "Word" of God. In other words, the blueprint charts for the "Word of God" were also the blueprints for the Temple of God in Israel. And, the blueprints of the Temple and the "Word" were also transparent and three dimensional.

What was even more unbelievable was that the class was being taught about "Word" (Torah) showing the inner make-up of the Temple of Israel, and the intricate dynamics of what was being shown through the Power Point blueprints was also demonstrating the inner make-up of a space ship as the "Word" of God. The Temple, and the Word of God were one and the same dynamic, and they were also a spaceship as seen in the blueprints, all in three dimensions. So, the Temple blueprints had diagrams of the "Word" of God as the Temple of Israel, and as a space ship physically being able to manifest as the Temple of Israel. Only, it all was also seen through the eyes of revelation.

As I began to realize the connection of all of what I was seeing, I was suddenly transported and found myself hovering over the actual Temple Mount of Israel. I was flying over Jerusalem in Israel and the Temple Mount, and hovering and watching all that was going on, only I was high up in the sky looking down, able to see the Temple Mount in the past, present, and future at the same time. I was hov-

*ering over the Temple Mount in Jerusalem and was seeing
all of it in the past, present and future all at the same time
while taking the Issachar class. As I descended to the Temple
Mount, I had flashes of revelation, all during the while the
course in the Issachar School was being taught. It wasn't a
vision, but more like a 3D experience simultaneously all at
once.*

*The revelation was that the Temple of Israel and my body
were literally connected as the same thing, and at the moment
I realized the connection in all that Dr. Heidler was teaching,
I knew that the blueprints used by Dr. Heidler were actually
about me - about all of us. The Temple, all of us, the "Word"
of God, and the spaceship were one and the same.*

*I was startled, amazed and wondering all I was expe-
riencing. Even as I began to ponder about all I was experiencing and realizing, the moment I pondered that the Temple
of Israel, and the "Word" of God was a spaceship and me,
I became the spaceship in a countdown for takeoff. Yes, I
was now where the Temple "was," on the Temple Mount
in Jerusalem, only I was the Temple and the Spaceship in a
countdown ready to be launched.*

*Before I could fight the idea with doubt, the countdown
was completed and I was launched into space directly from
where the Temple of Israel "was" on the Temple Mount in
Jerusalem. I was launched without being in the spaceship,
but I was actually the spaceship.*

*Only, in all of it, it was very real, and as I was the space-
ship in a countdown ready to be launched, and then launched
into space experiencing all of it in its drama of dynamic
anticipation and emotion, I was worshiping the Lord.*

*As I went higher and higher into space, the blue sky
turned to the deep dark recesses of space, and I passed
planets, stars, then galaxies, all the while I was worshiping
the Lord, as if my worship was the ignited fuel propelling,
and catapulting me into space. As I went deeper and deeper*

into space, I knew the Temple was my body, but the Temple of Israel was a real tangible place also, and also the blueprints and an intricate diagram Dr. Heidler was using that were the make-up of the "Word" in me that had revelation to cause us to become the Temple, as the spaceship (myself) was launched deeper and deeper into space into the Heavens of the Lord. I woke up praising the Lord. Actually, I woke up totally in awe of the Lord.

The dream was so realistic - one of the most realistic experiences I have ever had, almost realer than real life. It was some sort of supernatural fusion of revelation that was much more realistic than real life.

If you ever wondered about if God could read your mind, and then answer you by demonstrating His authority over everything that exists, I hope by reading this testimony that came as a night revelation from the Lord, you will have your "faith" strengthened. I also hope you will be in awe of the Lord of all, who is the Lord.

This dream was one of the most realistic of experiences – a realer than real life experience.

To this day, this dream works on me. Every time I think of what went on in this dream, I feel like my body, soul, mind and spirit are being transformed.

It is like being renewed into something fresh and new, almost like being transformed from a "glory" to another "Glory" in Jesus, all from this one night revelation.

But we all, with unveiled face, beholding as in a mirror the glory of the Lord, are being transformed into the same image from glory to glory, just as by the Spirit of the Lord (2 Corinthians 3:18 NKJV).

And do not be conformed to this world, but be transformed by the renewing of your mind, that you may prove what is that good and acceptable and perfect will of God (Romans 12:2 NKJV).

And God both raised up the Lord and will also raise us up by His power. (1 Corinthians 6:14, NKJV).

Or do you not know that your body is the temple of the Holy Spirit who is in you, whom you have from God, and you are not your own? For you were bought at a price; therefore glorify God in your body and in your spirit, which are God's. (1 Corinthians 6:19-20, NKJV).

It is remarkable and mysterious how the Lord speaks. A single "word," or sometimes in a timed long dream that seems long to us, but could be only a second in time, can speak a thousand revelations to us that will last all of our lives. And, in the dreaminess of it all, is the voice of God that does speak. Either way, the spoken word, or words of the Lord are bright lights in the night that can produce rivers of living water.

Call unto me, and I will answer thee, and show thee great and mighty things, which thou knowest not. (Jeremiah33:3, KJV)

Chapter 25

The Gift of Interpretation of God's Dreams Comes from God.

He reveals deep and hidden things; he knows what lies in darkness, And light dwells with him. (Daniel 2:22, NKJV)

The Holy Spirit, Jesus, and God the Father are the interpreters of dreams. God is the author and interpreter of our dreams. The trinity is the author of our dreams, and the source of the interpretation of our dreams. Ultimately, dreams are God's way of causing us to come into a closer relationship with Him. He has a dream for us to interpret and in the journey of life, God's dream for our life, can teach us, fulfill us, and make us whole in Him.

As we embrace God's interpretation of our life experiences, we come closer to His mysteries, and our interaction with others is made fuller, filled with healing and joy and happiness for everyone involved.

We should allow the Holy Spirit to help us interpret types and symbols in our dreams. Understanding the dreams we dream means we must allow the Holy Spirit to interpret our dreams for us.

Simply because, when we interpret our own dreams we think are for our own lives, without the Holy Spirit, we sometimes find out our dreams for ourselves have nothing to do with God's dreams for our life.

Similarly, when we dream a dream, we must surrender the interpretation of the dream to the Holy Spirit. When we do that, anything is possible, and sometimes believe me, the results are often mind blowing. And then you know, that you know, that you know, God is speaking.

When God Speaks, when God is involved in our interpretation anything is possible. The Gift of interpretation is a gift from God. Joseph and Daniel were given the gift of dream (night revelation) interpretation. Both, Daniel and Joseph understood that God was the author of dreams, and the interpreter of dreams. They took their dreams seriously.

And Jesus said, *"To you it has been given to know the mysteries of the kingdom of God, but to the rest it is given in parables, that Seeing they may not see, And hearing they may not understand."* (Luke 8:10, NKJV)

Daniel and Joseph in the Bible were dream interpreters. They were of excellence in spirit and God was with them. God gave them wisdom and knowledge because they knew that God was the author and interpreter of their dreams. Daniel was so aware of God's involvement in interpretation, and so respectful of the fact that God speaks in dreams; that, he praised God for giving him the wisdom to understand dreams.

As stated earlier, <u>thanking God</u> is something we should all do when we are given a dream from God, and receive understanding of what that dream means. It can never be understated, and our <u>thanking God</u> can never be too much. Through the gift of revelation and gift of unction, we are able to hear from God through the Holy Spirit, in order to interpret a dream or vision that does come from God. We should all be as grateful to God for His gift to us to interpret dreams as Daniel was.

We can never grow tired of thanking God enough, nor reading Daniel's praises of the Lord!

Then the secret was revealed to Daniel in a night vision.
So Daniel blessed the God of heaven.
Daniel answered and said:

Blessed be the name of God forever and ever,
For wisdom and might are His.
And He changes the times and the seasons;
He removes kings and raises up kings;
He gives wisdom to the wise
And knowledge to those who have understanding.
He reveals deep and secret things;
He knows what is in the darkness,
And light dwells with Him.
I thank You and praise You,
O God of my fathers;
You have given me wisdom and might,
And have now made known to me what we asked of You,
For You have made known to us the king's demand.
                                   (Daniel 2:19-23, NKJV)

Jesus gave us light - revelation, and is so filled with wisdom that even the darkness illuminates in the night with His light. He makes the darkness light. You know what happens when you have light introduced into the darkness? The light reveals what is in the darkness, forcing the darkness to become light, all the while revealing and exposing what has been hiding in the darkness. Wow, if we only could get a grip on this revelation!

Even the darkness is not dark to You, And the night is as bright as the day. Darkness and light are alike to You. (Psalm 139:12, ESV)

Therefore, Jesus is the interpreter of dreams. That is why it is important to remember, not every interpretation of a type and symbol from a dream will be the same meaning for every person who is seeking interpretation to their dream.

We should approach each dream, and it's meaning, according to the dreamer's dream language, as if the dream is owned by the dreamer, and not to try to impose our own language on others, even if we speak the same language, and have the same words to describe the dream.

After suggesting an interpretation, it is ultimately up to the dreamer to ask the Holy Spirit what a dream meant. Of course, that is not to say that there are not certain people given the gift of dream interpretation.

Certain people have been given by Jesus the ability to interpret dreams as demonstrated in the Bible by Joseph and Daniel. So the gift of interpretation, especially dreams, is a gift from God - Jesus, to be given out by Jesus, at His discretion and in His timing.

Chapter 26

What to do When Something is Fixed in the Heavens by God

There are times when the Lord can trust us enough to tell us something that is <u>fixed in the Heavens</u> that is going to happen. When the Lord knows of something fixed in the Heavens, it means that it **will** come to pass. At times, that which will come to pass is something very good, and at other times, the thing fixed in the Heavens is not so good. On occasion the Lord will speak these secrets in a dream. The Lord will not do anything unless he tells his prophets first.

Surely the Lord GOD does nothing, Unless He reveals His secret to His servants the prophets (Amos 3:7, NKJV)

Double Dreams - double blessings, or double trouble?

The same exact dream, on the same night, that you dream twice in that same night, is a night revelation where the Lord wants your attention about the matter and is possibly revealing a secret to you. He is speaking to you in the dream of something about to come to pass.

If you dream the same dream, or dream a dream similar to another dream you had, <u>but not</u> on the same night, but instead on consecutive nights, or periodically on different nights, that dream is a message telling you that you are not paying attention to God as He is trying to speak to you about what He is saying to you in night revelations. Or, perhaps you are not paying attention to something in your own life that is being shown to you in the dreams. He wants your attention to tell you something.

However, if you dream a dream, and you dreamed it twice <u>on the same night</u>, and you dream the same exact dream; that, is a totally different matter. Two dreams that are the same, that you receive on the same night, means; that what you saw in the dream, the events, the people, the happenings have been <u>set in the Heavens</u> and they will shortly come to pass. God is saying it will shortly come to pass.

And the dream was repeated to Pharaoh twice because the thing is established by God, and God will shortly bring it to pass (Genesis 41:32, NKJV)

In 2004, around the end of November, the Lord gave me a dream where I dreamed the same dream twice.

In the dream there was a big tsunami of water about to hit, and the only way people could be safe was to go to higher ground or be high up in buildings. I found myself watching from the upper floor of a building as the tsunami hit.

Although there was no indication in the dream as to where the tsunami was to hit, and I kind of felt that the dream implied a wave of the Holy Spirit coming, I did feel that the two dreams were some sort of warning of some kind of tsunami flood coming. But, I was not sure if the dream was symbolic or literal, as what went on in the dream could happen in real life but also could perhaps be symbolic. I felt like I was part of the dream, only at the same time watching in the dream. So, I was not sure if I should take the dream literally or symbolically, if it was about me, or those who were in the dream, but I did know something was coming.

I did tell several people about what I dreamed; however, the reception to what saw in the dream from those I spoke to was less that supportive; in that, they did not exactly believe me; that something was about to happen. However, I was in prayer about it because of what the Lord was showing me.

Only, I had never thought that an echo of what I dreamed would come to pass with such a direct shocking happening. Even to this day, I keep trying to see if anything at that time in my life was like being hit by a tsunami of water (wave of the Holy Spirit).

If you ever really have seen what went on in Banda Aceh, Indonesia, it was an event that was historical, and to its people, a frightening, life altering - changing event. It was not a month later, (after the two dreams) than one of the largest tsunami's to ever hit a population on the earth in modern times occurred on the 26th of December 2004 in Banda, Aceh, Indonesia. On that Sunday, December 26, 2004 an earthquake occurred beneath the surface of the ocean about 150 miles south east of Banda Aceh, Sumatra, Indonesia, and generated a tsunami that killed more than 280,000 people living near the coasts in, Thailand, Sri Lanka, Sumatra, and India, as well as the east coast of Africa. The earthquake, caused what was perhaps, one of the most devastating tsunamis ever recorded historically in modern times. The height of the wave was about 100 feet.

I remember telling people about the dreams, to my dismay of their somewhat silent, critical, disbelief; as, at the time, no one around me really felt dreams like that were of any significance. In fact, as the month progresses from that November, I think people were actually getting impatient with me and I found myself in a bit of a mess telling folk about the dreams.

When the Indonesian tsunami even occurred, I was shocked, and remained quiet for some time, but soon was mentioning it to folk. They believed me even less than before the event. Goes to show you, you will find various receptions to your dreams, and it is a wise thing to find people you trust to share your dreams with. But, that did not stop me from interceding (praying) for the people involved. I am writing this section of the book because Nick, at that time, was ministering the "Word" to me about Jesus, and was one of the very few people interested in what the Lord was saying to me in my dreams. Nick suggested for me to write about this to help us understand the level and nature of how God can possibly speak to us in our dreams.

We all have shaking dreams, and earth event dreams that almost all the time show us something that will happen to us, or is happening to us; but, on rare instances, the Lord might speak a dream to you that is about you and others like the dreams given and what happened after in 2004.

What you "can do" if you feel that you may have had two identical dreams in the same night is <u>to pray</u>. <u>Intercede</u> for what you saw; and, if what you saw was a good thing, intercede for it to come to pass showing the "Glory" of Jesus in all that will happen. Pray for the people involved, and know God is involved and aware of what is happening, and that God may be speaking to you, even speaking to you perhaps about a mystery or a secret of something that is about to happen that is set in the Heavens to happen, such as a natural event occurring.

These two same dreams on the same night gave me an awareness of the sovereignty of God, and the impression that God is very aware of everything that shall come to pass. It is a sobering and mysterious dilemma to pray and ponder about.

✓ Two dreams that are the same, that you receive on the same night, means; that what you saw in the dream, the events, the people, the happenings have been set in the Heavens and they will shortly come to pass.

Chapter 27

Pizza Dreams:
When You Think What You Ate at Night Caused Your Dream

12-03-13

When you think what you ate at night caused your dream, do not necessarily toss the food out. Should we always toss out our dreams when we think they are from what we ate at night? Unique and sometimes odd dreams that we think come from excessively hot foods, or the just odd foods we eat, are often times referred to as Pizza Dreams.

Do not just throw out your dreams because you think you ate something at night that may have caused the dream, especially if you are dreaming about food, or other funny, seemingly irrelevant things. The Lord often times uses the foolish to confound the wise, and certain dreams could very likely be talking to you profoundly, and you do not even know it. Jesus has a wonderful sense of humor, and is very aware of your family background, dream language, and personal understanding of the way you see contemporary life and live it. Jesus will <u>challenge you</u> by talking to you about profound things in a seemingly foolish way if you are operating from a "religious" type of pharisaic spirit of legalism. He will use the foolish to confound you!

That is not to say that, perhaps some of the dreams we have are not triggered by abnormally hot foods, prescription drugs, excessive sugar, too much soda, etc... However, often the simplest dream with food in it can be a way Jesus may want to speak to us. Sometimes the food itself is symbolic of the region of the world the food comes from, or the things we are taking into us like what we are reading, watching on TV, speaking about, or what we are listening to.

Dream:

I was stopping at a donut pastry store to get a cup of coffee and a donut (something sweet), only when I went into the store, the only thing that was on the shelf, where the donuts were supposed to be, were Italian cannoli. Only these cannoli were huge, I mean they looked like the size of shoe boxes about 16" x 8" x 8". The clerk who was there said to me: "Can I get you a cannoli?" A little shocked, I asked the clerk if he had any smaller cannoli than what they (the store) was offering to me? He didn't exactly respond, but implied that they had regular cannoli. "But I would like a cup of coffee" I thought and said. All the while thinking: "that is some cannoli, seriously rich, and there is just no way to eat that thing in one sitting or even a few sittings". I was also thinking: "What in the world"? I have never seen a cannoli baked that size, and so big to actually eat, in my entire life I had never heard of such a thing! Talk about a sweet very, very, rich thing!

The clerk then said to me: "Do you want a small cup of coffee or a large cup of coffee?" I said: "a large cup of coffee thank you." So he handed me the large cup of coffee. Then another clerk to the right near the door, who was sampling spinach pie said to me: "Would you like a piece of this pie". I responded by accepting the sample he offered me, and I went on my way with a cannoli, cup of coffee and a piece of the spinach pie. Then I woke up.

"Holy Cannoli"!

Ok, now in this dream we have to decide whether or not it is worth pondering, or could it be from something we ate that was Italian food.

Only, several hours after this night revelation, I received a phone call from Eagles Wings Ministries. A team member had asked me a question. She asked: *"Would you respectfully consider helping Eagles Wings Ministries with the State of Pennsylvania mobilizing, and serving coordinators for the "Day to Pray for the Peace of Jerusalem and Eagles Wings Ministries Jerusalem Projects?"*

There was no real context to cause me to have the dream, thus the dream was a prophetic dream where Jesus was speaking directly to me, or his angels where. This was regarding something about to be presented to me, and there was clear direction for me to follow based on the questions Jesus asked me in the dream. Often times God (Jesus) will ask us questions in order for us to expand our understanding of events, situations, or concepts.

Based on this dream, I knew the Lord had spoken to me already earlier. And, so I moved into responding to the call from the Lord to work aligned with Eagles Wings - DPPJ and the team that soon developed after.

As you can see, the Lord has a sense of humor (in this instance), and an understanding of our situations far in advance of our knowing about them.

Let us take a look at the interpretation of this night revelation. Oh, first let's take a look at the plural of cannoli, just so your sense of the many cannoli is appeased. "Cannoli" is actually the plural for "cannolo, or the word for "tube" in Italian. Ok, now that we have that settled, let's take a look at the interpretation: a huge cannoli is just not what one would expect and are very rich. A regular cannoli is a rich sweet thing one can eat; but, a huge cannoli that is 16" x 8" x 8" is a bit surreal as, I do not think they actually exist. (Maybe they do, but I have never seen one).

This makes the dream symbolic, as since it does not exist in real life, the dream now enters into the realm of a symbolic dream. A huge cannoli is a funny thing to dream about and a huge cannoli is overwhelming if you were to consider eating it. At first, you realize you either need help eating it or need to serve it to many, or you will have to take your time with it. It is also so rich that it makes you feel full even before you take a bite, or bite into it (which is a metaphor). This shows Jesus has a sense of humor, and a loving joking personality in this night revelation.

Having the option of choosing a small cup of coffee, or a large cup of coffee is symbolic (remember, huge cannoli really do not often exist in real life therefore the dream is symbolic) so the coffee is symbolic and represents something that stimulates and refreshes me in my dream language. The larger cup of coffee would imply that I was asked by the Lord if I would prefer just a small amount of action and stimulation in the Holy Spirit, or a larger amount, meaning He was implying that both kinds of stimulation will come from the participation in what was to come my way.

Now the spinach pie and the direct question from Jesus implies that: the Lord wanted to know if I wanted to experience a "piece of the pie" (which is a metaphorical contemporary pun that means "*do you want to be a part of something*"). Something that, if you partake of it would be like eating my spinach that would make me strong, almost like Popeye the Sailor; who, when he ate his spinach was given supernatural strength beyond the normal, to defeat Brutus the bully or brute. Of course, this requires an understanding of metaphor through a personal dream language to realize it.

Spinach is very good for us, and it can strengthen us. Although the symbols are a bit universal in a contemporary language of modern day, the dream was the Lord's way of speaking to me to encourage me through humor, and something that was part of the cultural upbringing in my life, and perhaps other's lives as well. Jesus was asking me, hinting to me to participate, but had a loving sense of humor about it, because the dynamics of the war over Israel and walking out "a piece of the pie", so to speak can sometimes get riddled with all sorts of warfare, even warfare about how people perceive God through their own minds or their perceptions.

So, the Lord was asking me in a loving and humorous way:

"*if I wanted to be part of, [do I want a piece of] something that would give me a supernatural strength, perhaps even to defeat bullies, that is a very sweet, and a special rich huge thing that would stimulate me; or, just choose the small coffee, a small bit of something sweet; or, nothing sweet, and continue on my way without experiencing a "piece of the pie"?*

But God has chosen the foolish things of the world to put to shame the wise, and God has chosen the weak things of the world to put to shame the things which are mighty (1 Corinthians 1:27, NKJV).

Chapter 28

Winebibbers, Hauling Oats, Jackasses, and Prostitutes
Oh my gosh, is this really God speaking?

Jesus may come to you in ways you least expect it! God may speak to you in ways as to shock you into paying attention!

Yep, tell your average Pastor about those exciting themes and you may end up in Bible deliverance 101, till they try to cast the uncastable out of you, reteach you how to talk Christianeeze, and, well, maybe if you're really lucky, find all their efforts hopeless. Thank God, I seldom hang around just average Pastors. Don't know too many of them.

The reality of night revelation is: Jesus may come to you in ways you least expect it, in incredible ways you may hardly believe. He may show up as a Winebibber prodding and egging you on, to motivate you, or a dream might show you your Pastor running off with a Prostitute (symbolic of Jesus wanting you to pray for your pastor that he does not prostitute some concept in the church). Or, have a donkey speak to you, or refer to a donkey as an ass. Yes, He may literally call a donkey an ass or a Jackass in your dream. A winebibber, drinks a lot of wine (symbolic of perhaps being Holy Spirit filled with dunamis) and winebibbers can be a friend of publicans and sinners *(Luke 7:34),* and the symbolic character of a winebibber is just like what Jesus would want us to do to hint to us, prodding us on to "Go" and take the Gospel of the Kingdom to everyone, not just those living fair to decent lives, but those who need it the most.

The reality of the way the Lord may speak is related to getting our attention, or even speaking to us in a reference to a past, present, or future through language vernacular.

Example: The word donkey, the way we know it, did not exactly exist in Jesus' time, and in many Bibles from the past the word "donkey" was represented by the word "ass". And, an "ass" may refer to a symbolic concept such as a beast of burden - donkey, an intercessor burdened by the weight of their concern, or a Hebrew meaning of the word Issachar. Or, there may be a person who operates in the "Issachar" anointing whose name is Jack, and you may know them enough that the Lord wants you to warn them they are not acting properly, thus the term "Jack Ass" could be used to shock you into responding, or because people are calling the person a "Jack Ass" behind their back, and the Lord is concerned, and wants you to pray for them. A male donkey or ass is called a "Jack", so the Lord could be referring to someone you know, who is a man that is carrying a great burden of intercession.

The curious reason the Lord might speak in such a shocking way, might also be related to the fact that: He wants our attention, and we could be limited in who we

179

can take that type of revelation to (or God places us in a boundary by the very nature of the kind of language we can, or cannot communicate with. In other words, the Lord has us in a specific boundary he wants us to remain in. He wants us to remain in a certain sphere of authority - boundary, keeping us in check, so we don't take the information to the wrong people, in the wrong place, at the wrong time.

There is another reason the Lord might speak to you in such shocking ways, and that is <u>you may have a "religious" spirit</u>, or what some would term as operating under the effects of a pharisaic spirit that is in you; which is limiting your ability to move forward in what Jesus has for you. That spirit in you may also be harming others in your sphere of influence, through its limiting dynamic, and the projection of a control that could curse others due to a false perspective implanted in you from legalistic absolute perspectives that are keeping things in you bound.

Dream:

I was leaving my night revelation from an auditorium area; when, Daryl Hall came up to me with an ushers basket. (Daryl Hall from the musical band Hall and Oates) He was obviously trying to catch me before I left my dream and gestured to me - handing me the ushers basket and said: "Do you want to usher?" hoping I would not leave the dream and instead stay to usher.

Thus was the ending to a rather "mind blowing" dream in which the Lord showed me later His amazing dimension of secret secrets that folk think He would never tell (But, those secret secrets revealed in that dream will remain secret). Jesus can tell you the most incredible secrets! Yes, "you", that's right, He can tell "you" His secrets! A portion of the dream's revelation however, I feel I can tell you to build your faith in Jesus Christ and His dynamic of revelation as we are encouraged to <u>Dream God's Dreams</u> for our life.

"The secret things belong to the LORD our God, but those things which are revealed belong to us and to our children forever, that we may do all the words of this law. (Deuteronomy 29:29, NKJV).

You might ask: "why Hall and Oates"? Well I did, and although I had not been following their musical genius for some time, I loved, and still like their music, and when I looked up the musical band on the internet, I was seriously shocked to find out Daryl Hall had just finished an album entitled *Can't Stop Dreaming*.

You see, there was a time when my dreams became dreams that I followed and lived for; to the dismay and opposition of the belief of so very many, to the opposing mocking spirit of some, to the oppressive self-righteous spirit of others, and even the competitive envy of others, except my closest friends.

So, Jesus encouraged me in this dream by telling me: that I *Can't Stop Dreaming*! Don't stop dreaming, keep dreaming! That, it was important for me that I continue to dream, and that it was also important to Him that: "you *Can't Stop Dreaming*". And, He was funny teasing me about it as well, telling me, that I seem to not be able to stop dreaming; that, I *Can't Stop Dreaming*. He probably loved the "sound" of the music on that album too.

But, get this, not only was I told that: "I *Can't Stop Dreaming*"; but, the Lord was asking me if I wanted to "usher" in the Harvest. Wow...like "The Harvest", or as a simile in sound from the words Hall and Oates would imply – to be hauling oats. And, did you know, there just might be a specific Country the Lord is going to begin to usher in - to haul in the oats of "The Great Harvest"?

There is no rule that Jesus has to speak to us in a way that is proper according to our own "religious" perspective. Jesus, if He wants, can communicate in the way He did when he was on earth, according to the language and understanding of His day, and if He does, then there is a real good reason for it. It is not arbitrary and random the way God will speak to us. It is deliberate! There is definitely a reason for what God does, and for the way He says things.

Simply put, Jesus may speak to us in such ways as to <u>shock us into paying attention,</u> and challenge us to look at ourselves, in order for us to question, of what "spirit", and perspective, do we really perceive things from?

Chapter 29

Are All Dreams from God?

Not all dreams are from God. Some dreams are natural processes of our day and life experiences. That does not necessarily mean that they should be ignored. As I stated earlier, one of the best gems of wisdom for me came from Dr. Chuck Pierce who suggested that: *"A dream not interpreted is like a letter not opened and not read."*

Some dreams are our own nature of self-edification and could be echoing the state and nature of our desires in our natural person. Our desires unchecked by the Holy Spirit can become soul desires expressed in dreams and visions of the night (Like day dreaming about ourselves and our own self-importance).

If you suspect that you are having these kinds of dreams, pray to the Lord that you will not be deceived by your own self, and that you will not be a victim to self-deception. Or, that the spirit of self-edifying deception would not be allowed to affect you. Pray that you will have the courage to submit your desires to the Lord to edit your destiny the way He saw it before you were born. Then submit your desires to Jesus.

Also, some dreams could simply be from spirits other than the Holy Spirit, and some of those spirits are working for the enemy. However, if you are truly are Holy Spirit-filled, and not just a Christian by title in what you believe ...

... having a form of godliness but denying its power. And from such people turn away! (2 Timothy 3:5, NKJV)

it is sometimes hard for spirits other than the Holy Spirit to enter your dream life; because, spirits and demons run from the Holy Spirit and Holy Spirit's shield of your "faith." Your shield of the Holy Spirit (shield of faith) has to be maintained though. That means living in alignment with Heaven and God's will for your life, and not allowing the enemy to get through your shield of faith to have any claim on you through sin.

Another thing I learned from Dr. Chuck Pierce about our demeanor before we go to sleep was really a revelation of importance:

"If you go to sleep angry, with hating and bitterness, or with a hatefully vexed spirit, you can be demonized, and you will end up needing deliverance."

There is no way to be protected because your bitterness can cause your shield of faith to be lowered and your vexation may very well have run off the angels that do protect you. Not to mention, you could be running off the Holy Spirit or grieving the Holy Spirit. So, even if you are Holy Spirit filled, you can be demonized if you go to sleep with vexation and hatred in your heart.

Another way you can be fooled by a dream is to believe a dream from the enemy is really from God, or believe a dream from God is really a dream from the enemy. This can happen by not seeking help or mentoring from someone under proper aligned authority. That means you should try to find someone who has been around longer than you, who has experience in matters of the Holy Spirit (like your pastor, apostolic authority and covering, or simply a leader in your cell group).

If you are a leader always leading, and not willing to learn and be taught, you might also have the same problems of visitations from spirits other than the Holy Spirit. An un-teachable spirit is no different than Lucifer's self-edifying spirit of exclamation of being like God, and claiming of knowing everything. Thus, you could be echoing the enemy. If you are echoing the enemy, you will invite him into your bed with you at night.

The better aligned and covered by authority that actually wants to protect you, the cleaner, clearer, and more Holy Spirit filled your dreams will be. However, if you are covered by authority that does not want to protect you (like King Saul who had authority over David, and as David did not want to wear Saul's armor to protect himself even before he went to slay Goliath), if for a reason you are covered by authority that is not interested in protecting you, or if you are not in a correct fivefold dynamic of foundational Apostolic and Prophetic alignment, you could find yourself with a less than pure dream life.

Even the leaders, pastors, or authority you place yourself under will at times be wrestling with the enemy in their night revelations due to the way they approach their personal placement and alignment, and their understanding of the order of their alignment with Heaven, as well as, with each other in their own wine skins. That's not to say this is always the case though.

If you are a Holy Spirit-filled Christian, but your shield of faith in the Holy Spirit was let down, the dreams that may be from spirits other than the Holy Spirit, and, or, spirits working for the enemy; can sometimes reveal what the enemy is up to and plotting. The best way to discern if your dream is from the enemy; is, to ask yourself: if what you were shown echo's the character and principals in the Bible, or the message echo's the character of Jesus. If not, the enemy may be trying to fool you.

Also, as mentioned earlier, if your dreams are in black and white, instead of having color in them, the Lord may be trying to tell you that what you saw in your dream (theater of the mind), in your dream movie displayed in black and white is what the enemy is up to and what he is doing. Remember, all spectrums of color and light - life emanate from God.

It is never the intention of Jesus to torment us in the night, but He is always looking to bless us, unctioning us in our dreams to move forward, delivering us from our issues, protecting us, and moving us into a whole and fulfilled destiny in Shalom.

Whatever you do, review your day with the Lord before you go to sleep, and ask for forgiveness if you feel you may have not walked correctly. And, ask for help from Jesus to be more like Him, rejecting the devil, and moving far from echoing the nature of the devil into reflecting His light. And, by all means, do not go to sleep hating and angry.

Chapter 30

And It Shall Come to Pass!
(Joel 2:28, NKJV)

And it shall come to pass afterward
That I will pour out My Spirit on all flesh;
Your sons and your daughters shall prophesy,
Your old men shall dream dreams,
Your young men shall see visions.

(Joel 2:28, NKJV)

Each of us hears from God in our own language; as, God will meet us where we are, in what we are doing, and in how we do speak in our language. God speaks sometimes in ways we would never expect.

Sometimes we can easily understand Him, and other times we must hunt for the treasure He had hidden for us in the dream. In hunting for the treasure, God may want us to encounter things, events, people, in the journey (hunt), only to facilitate further His purposes in Kingdom advancement "in His timing". Sometimes, hunting for the answer can place us in God's timing. So, the hunt may be God's way of regulating time and the release of the revelation. We do receive revelation in part, and in God's timing, <u>where</u> He wants to release His word, and <u>when</u> He wants to speak.

When the corporate "body" of Christ is about to assemble, or is assembling to march forward. Each dream, "Word", or vision pieced together will reveal by confirmation that the Lord is speaking to the "body".

For we know in part and we prophesy in part (1 Corinthians 13:9, NKJV)

Dreams are God's way to allow us to understand it is ok to dream (metaphor), especially if the dreams we dream are <u>God's Dream</u> for our lives and others. We have an awesome God that blesses and judges righteously, and sometimes God will tell us what He is about to do through a dream. And, sometimes Jesus will tell to tell others what He is about to do, while other times Jesus will want us to wait till He is ready to march forward before He allows us to know the revelation from Him. And, sometimes God does not want us to tell anyone what He said. That is one of the great mysteries of life posed in a simple question:

"are we willing to listen to God and be obedient to His will, sometimes against all odds"?

God is ultimately interested in displaying His LOVE, His GLORY as LOVE, and has chosen His son Jesus to reveal His Kingdom to us, and give us the way to live forever through Jesus. Eternity awaits those who believe Jesus is God's son, and God the Father makes it possible to live forever, by accepting His son, and learning from the character and example of Jesus.

And, one of the most remarkable ways Jesus communicates with us is through our dreams; because,

Jesus wants us to dream, and to fulfill God's dreams for our life that was seeded in the Heavens even before we were born. God knitted in us a "glory" that "is" Jesus in our beings, and that "Glory" can manifest His LOVE which is the ultimately an expression of God's dream for us, as we all are ***Dreaming God's Dreams.***

Conclusion

The Most Important Dream of Your Life

If after reading this book, you are curious about Jesus, or you want to know more about Jesus, and would like to let Jesus help you by actively becoming part of your life, the below prayer may very well be the most important prayer you will ever pray. This prayer can start you on the dream of a lifetime; one that happens both when you are asleep and awake.

To allow Jesus to be in your heart, and be the Light that guides you throughout your life, **please say this prayer:**

Lord, Father in Heaven, in the Name of Jesus, I come to you asking you to hear my prayer. Can you help me become a whole person in you? I pray and ask Jesus to be part of my life, and to be Lord over my life.

I believe it in my heart, so I say it with my mouth: "Jesus is Love, and has been raised from the dead, and is your Son. At this moment in my life, I want to state with my heart; that, I believe in Jesus, and want to make Jesus Lord in my life. At this moment, I make Him the Lord over my life and ask Him to help me.

I ask you, Jesus, to forgive me of the sins I have committed throughout my life. I am willing to change. Jesus, come into my heart. I believe at this moment that I am saved by allowing You to be in me - to come into my heart. I say it now: I am new and reborn in you Jesus. I am a Christian. I am a child of Almighty God the Father. Amen!

Thank you God, for making me a child in Your Kingdom, and allowing me to receive the saving grace of Your son Jesus. Thank you Jesus! Amen!

If you said this prayer sincerely with an open heart, and would like to know further, more about your new walk in Jesus, below is a website you can contact that can help you know Jesus further. It would be a good idea to go get yourself a Bible and just start reading it from its beginning in Genesis.

Even if you do not understand what you may be reading in the Bible, keep reading the stories, asking Jesus to help you understand. And, by all means, if you so would like, find a local Christian church, worship center, or ministry of which you can become a part.

If you would like help in your new walk with Jesus, and you don't have a local place to worship and pray, you can contact New Covenant Christian Community (www.nc4.org) and they will be able to help you get started in your walk with the Lord.

Congratulations and blessings to you in your new walk with Christ Jesus!

You shall receive power when the Holy Spirit has come upon you!

But you shall receive power when the Holy Spirit has come upon you; and you shall be witnesses to Me in Jerusalem, and in all Judea and Samaria, and to the end of the earth (Acts 1:8, NKJV).

But you, beloved, building yourselves up on your most holy faith, praying in the Holy Spirit (Jude 1:20, NKJV).

If after reading this book, you are curious about the Holy Spirit of Jesus, believe in Jesus, and have accepted Jesus into your heart; and, would like to let Jesus fill you with His Holy Spirit, and help you by actively becoming part of your life, the prayer below will allow Holy Spirit of Jesus to be in your heart, and be the light that guides you throughout your life, through the power of Holy Spirit. (You will know, that you know, that you know, when the Holy Spirit has come upon you).

Warning: This power of the Holy Spirit, although available to all, is for those who have already been born into a new life by receiving Jesus Christ as their Lord and Savior. Otherwise, if you choose to call upon the Holy Spirit and say this prayer, you need to know that the Holy Spirit is Jesus. In fact, if you do not believe that Jesus is God, and is your savior, this prayer may change a few things in your life, and possibly, in some cases, could realign your life a bit, even shake a few things up in your life by shifting them. That's if you do not believe in Jesus and say this prayer. The Spirit of Jesus is gentle and kind, and always loves when you want more of His Holy Spirit. So, if you have not received

Christ Jesus as your personal mentor and savior, and do not want Jesus in your life, nor believe in Jesus, stop now, and think about it a bit before you may say this prayer.

Come Holy Spirit; fill me with your Love.

"Jesus, thank you for forgiving my sins because you died on the cross for me. Thank you for allowing everyone who believes in you, to receive your Holy Spirit. I am asking, and desire to be filled with your Holy Spirit, to have your Holy Spirit in me, and to fill my heart up with your Holy Spirit and with your love. I desire to know what your will is for my life through your Holy Spirit in me.

Jesus you promised; that: "if I ask in your name anything that is according to your will for my life, and if I believe that I will receive it, then I can have

what I ask for and it is mine. Therefore, I ask, in your name, for the fullness and power of your Holy Spirit to come into my heart and upon me right now. I receive your Holy Spirit by faith, and will wait upon you Lord.

I thank you for answering this prayer to fill me with your Holy Spirit. Please use me for your purposes and your glory as I fulfill your will for my life.

In Jesus' name, I ask for your Holy Spirit, and wait on you to receive your Holy Spirit. I receive the Holy Spirit by my faith in you Jesus. Thank You Jesus,
Amen."!

If you said this prayer sincerely with an open heart, and would like to know further, more about this power in your new walk with the Holy Spirit – Jesus, below is a website you can contact that can help you know the Holy Spirit, the fruit, and gifts of the Holy Spirit further. It would be a good idea to go get yourself a

Bible and just start reading it from its beginning in Genesis. Even if you don't understand what you may be reading, keep reading the stories asking the Holy Spirit to help you understand.

And, by all means, if you so would like, find a local Holy Spirit filled Christian church, worship center, or ministry that allows, accepts and operates in the Holy Spirit, that you can become a part of.

Again, If you would like help in your new walk with the Holy Spirit, and you don't have a local place to worship that allows the Holy Spirit to operate, or allows you pray in the Holy Spirit; that, does allow the gifts of the Holy Spirit in you to be released, you are more than welcome to contact New Covenant Christian Community (www.nc4.org) and they may be able to help you get started in your walk and understanding of the Holy Spirit (Jesus).

Bibliography Comments

This is a list of ministries, books, teachers and teachings that have influenced me over the years in regards to dreams. The material in this book cannot be assumed to be attributed to any one reference, ministry, person, or teaching unless mentioned as such. Much of what I learned, in part, was assimilated in my hunger for the understanding my dreams. With that stated, the end notes here are listed to provide a more complete picture of my background in formalized education about night revelation, and as reference, in part, to the material in this book.

Bibliography

Breathitt, Barbie. *Dream Encounters*, (Parts 1-12), ©2006, Breath of the Spirit Ministries, Inc. North Richland Hills, Texas

Bydeley, Steve & Dianne. *Dream Dreams*, ©2002, Essence Publishing, Canada

Cross Publications, *The Eight Beatitudes of Jesus*, Cross Publications of Savannah, Georgia (www.jesus-christsavior.net)

Day to Pray for the Peace of Jerusalem ©. *Day to Pray (DPPJ)*, Jerusalem Projects, Eagles Wings Ministries, (www.daytopray.com), Rev. Robert Stearns, Pastor Jack Hayford, Rodlyn Park

Engle, Lou. *God is Stirring a Holy Prayer Storm - Now is the time to Pray your Dream into Existence! Part 1*, © 2008, When God's Dreams Become Your Reality

Goll, James. *Experiencing Dreams and Visions*, (Parts 1-15), ©2002, Encounters Network, Tulsa, Oklahoma

Groblewski, Pastors Jack & Trish. *Pastor Jack's Dream, Pastor Trish's Dream,* © 2010, NC4, New Covenant Christian Community, Bethlehem, Pa (Advisors & Encouragement to actually write this book)

Hall, Daryl. *Can't Stop Dreaming* © 1996, solo album, originally released in Japan and as a Limited Collector's Edition in 1996, released in the USA on June 10, 2003

Heidler, Robert. *The Gift of Interpretation,* Dr. Chuck Pierce, Barbie Breathett, © 2007, The Issachar School, Denton, Texas

The Issachar School. Denton, Texas, © Glory of Zion Ministries
Jackson, John Paul. *Understanding Dreams and Visions,* Streams Ministries, ©1999, Sutton, New Hampshire

Killian, Rev. Wayne. *The Newman Center,* Lehigh University, Bethlehem, Pa, Catholic Campus Ministries of the Diocese of Allentown, Pa.

Nouwen, Henri, J.M. *In the Name of Jesus, Reflections on Christian Leadership,* © 1989, The Crossroads Publishing Company, New York, NY

Pierce, Chuck. *Taking the Night,* Dr. Robert Heidler, Jane Hamon, Barbie Breathett, Eitan Shishkoff, © 2007, Glory of Zion Ministries, Denton, Texas

Pierce, Chuck. *Understanding and Interpreting Dreams,* Dr. Barbara Wentroble, Dr. Robert Heidler, © 2003, Denton, Texas

Quasten, Rev. Johanness. *St. Gregory of Nyssa*, Rev. Joseph C. Plumpe, The Lord's Prayer and The Beatitudes. Ancient Christian Writers, Paulist Press, Mahwah, New Jersey. © 1954

Riffel, Rev. Herman. *Christian Dream Interpretation*, (Parts 1 & 2), © Protected, Re-Published, © 2010 Connectivity Group LLC, MD

Segar, Elzie Crisler. *Popeye*, Thimble Theatre, King Features, © January 17, 1929

Tate, Anne. Glory of Zion Ministries International, Denton, Texas, (an encouragement during the writing of this book)

Westgate, Nick. *Nick's Dream*, © 2010, Bridging the Gap, Bethlehem, Pennsylvania

Wikipedia, online encyclopedia (www.wikipedia.org)

Special Thanks

Trish Groblewski, NC4, New Covenant Christian Community in Bethlehem, Pennsylvania. (She encouraged me to write this book)

Pastor Jack Groblewski, NC4, New Covenant Christian Community in Bethlehem, Pennsylvania. (For his help, advice, and encouraged while writing this book)

Dr. Chuck Pierce (Chancellor), Dr. Robert Heidler (Dean), and the staff of the Issachar School at Glory of Zion Ministries.

Anne Tate, Glory of Zion Ministries International in Denton, Texas. (She provided and was a source of encouragement during the writing of this book)

Nick Westgate and Family, Bridging the Gap, Bethlehem, Pennsylvania (Faithful friend, always an encouragement in my walk with Jesus)

Steve & Dianne Bydeley, Lapstone Ministries, Canada (who were there to help me understand my dreams when few were there to help, or even wanted to listen)

Rev. Wayne Killian, The Newman Center, Lehigh University in Bethlehem, Pennsylvania, Catholic Campus Ministries of the Diocese of Allentown,

Pennsylvania. (one of the first people to recognize I was hearing from the Lord through my dreams)

And, as always:
Frank and Marie Donnangelo (my parents), who without their support, this manuscript would not have been possible.

Dreaming God's Dreams

The opinions and understanding of dreams pre-sented in this book is from personal revelation in my walk with the Lord Jesus Christ. In no way do the people, churches and ministries mentioned in this book have any responsibility for what has been presented. They were mentioned to assist in understanding that which was presented.

David Michael Donnangelo

Education

David Michael Donnangelo is a professional artist & writer, and a graduate of *Moravian College & Theological Seminary*, Bethlehem, Pa. with a B.S. degree in Studio Arts.

Moravian College is a Liberal Arts College, and the sixth oldest College in America, tracing its roots back to the **Herrnhut Moravians** from Germany. The seminary also traces back to: two boy's schools established in 1742 - 1743, and to Countess Benigna von Zinzendorf, daughter of **Count Nikolaus Ludwig von Zinzendorf.**

David received ministry training with certification of completion from Chuck Pierce's **Issachar School,** Glory of Zion, Denton, Texas. **The Issachar School** © was founded by Dr. Robert Heidler (Dean), and Dr. Chuck Pierce (Chancellor). The Issachar School is a regional affiliate of Wagner Leadership Institute, and Global Spheres Inc.

David's education also includes:

The Baum School of Fine Art
Temple University – Tyler School of Art
Pennsylvania Governor's School for the Arts.
The Barnes Foundation – Violette de Mazia
Foundation

Illustration for Dante's *Divine Comedy* (Heaven)
By: David Michael Donnangelo

www.contemporaryfineart.org

http://www.contemporaryfineartandgifts.com/
NEW-FEATURED-POSTER.html

The religious symbolist artwork of David Michael Donnangelo can best be understood and appreciated if it is viewed as a contemporary "link" in the sacred chain of the mystical-symbolist school of painters. In particular, Donnangelo's work brings to mind the esoteric and historical master works of Van Eyck, Bosch,

William Blake, Gustave Dore', Max Beckman, Carlos Cara, and most recently the illustrious Balthus.

The works of David Michael Donnangelo, beyond, perhaps, all other contemporary artists, provides us with a unique blend of penetrating visual insight into our modern metaphysical and social dilemmas, while at the same time, demonstrating extraordinarily high-levels of technical skill and achievement.

In his most recent narrative painting Donnangelo examines and explicates the morally complex inter-play of race, gender, and class in post modern America. The artist provides us with a sobering vision, redolent with personal meanings and reflective of the best tradi-tions of the social realists, bringing to mind the master works of George Grosz, Otto Dix, and the psycholog-ical narrative insights of Georgio De Chirico, Balthus, and Rene' Magritte.

Arthur Eisenbuch P.H.D
New York City

Psalm 18

CPSIA information can be obtained at www.ICGtesting.com
Printed in the USA
BVOW04s2045131013

333570BV00002B/3/P